# LEARNING TO TRUST YOURSELF

A JOURNEY TO SELF-DISCOVERY AND
EMPOWERMENT

DR. MICHAEL J. DUCKETT

# COPYRIGHT

# CONTENTS

## Dear Reader,

The substance of a message far outweighs its length. This book has been purposefully crafted in a concise format, designed to deliver essential information without unnecessary verbosity, reflecting my signature writing style. Many readers have found value in this approach, as it enables a swift and meaningful engagement with the content, free from unnecessary filler. In a world saturated with extraneous information, most individuals seek clarity and efficiency in reading. I believe you will find this endeavor of mine to be a valuable addition to your life.

## DISCLAIMER

The information presented in this book is not intended for diagnosing, treating, or healing any health condition. Instead, this book serves as an educational tool to enlighten readers about the boundless opportunities in life. While the stories and events in the book are rooted in reality, certain elements have been fictionalized for educational purposes, and specific names have been altered to safeguard individuals' privacy.

## CONTACT INFO

Upgradinglife.com

425 E. Crossville Road, Suite 101

Roswell, GA 30075

# INTRODUCTION

*Learning to Trust Yourself*

In the tapestry of human existence, a thread is woven delicately, yet profoundly, into the very fabric of our being. It's a thread often overlooked, overshadowed by the cacophony of external expectations and the relentless pursuit of validation from others. This thread is self-trust, a core pillar upon which our authentic selves are built. It's the foundation upon which our personal growth, happiness, and fulfillment rest.

In this book, we embark on a transformative journey that delves deep into the essence of self-trust and explores the remarkable transformation it can bring to your life. It is a journey of rediscovering the power within yourself, embracing your authenticity, and cultivating a profound belief in your own abilities.

## Defining Self-Trust

To understand the significance of self-trust, let's begin by defining it. Self-trust is the unwavering belief in your capacity to make decisions, take actions, and navigate life's challenges in a way that aligns with your true self and values. It's the inner knowing that you can rely on your judgment, intuition, and abilities, even when uncertain.

Imagine a life where you trust yourself completely and move forward with confidence, secure in the knowledge that you are the compass guiding your own path. A life where you embrace your unique qualities, make choices that resonate with your heart and stand tall in the face of adversity. Such a life is not a distant dream; it is within your reach, waiting to be cultivated and nurtured.

## Why Self-Trust Matters

The significance of self-trust cannot be overstated. It is the cornerstone of authentic living. When you trust yourself, you pave the way for a life that is true to your values, passions, and aspirations. You liberate yourself from the stifling grip of self-doubt, societal expectations, and the need for external validation.

Self-trust is the force that propels you to set audacious goals, face your fears head-on, and persist in the face of setbacks. It empowers you to listen to your inner voice, to honor your intuition, and to make choices that reflect your deepest desires. With self-trust as your guiding star, you can weather life's storms with grace and emerge stronger, wiser, and more resilient.

Consider, for a moment, the ripple effect of self-trust. As you nurture this inner belief, you become an inspiration to others. Your journey towards authenticity and self-trust becomes a beacon of hope for those around you, encouraging them to embark on their own paths of self-discovery and empowerment.

## The Consequences of Self-Doubt

On the flip side, self-doubt can be a relentless adversary. It erodes your confidence, stifles your potential, and imprisoned you within the confines of your comfort zone. It leads to hesitation, procrastination, and missed opportunities. Self-doubt can create a dissonance between who you are and who you wish to become.

In the following pages, we will explore the origins of self-doubt and how it can hold you back. We will unveil the power of self-awareness, self-compassion, and intuition as tools to dismantle the fortress of doubt. We will journey together through setting authentic goals, embracing failure, and nurturing self-confidence.

This book is not a magical incantation that erases self-doubt overnight. It is a roadmap—a guide through the landscapes of self-discovery and growth. It offers insights, exercises, and stories illuminating the path towards self-trust and authenticity. A companion walks beside you as you uncover the layers of doubt, fear, and insecurity, revealing the radiant core of self-trust that has always resided within you.

As you turn the pages of this book, remember that your journey is unique. Your experiences, challenges, and victories are your own. The insights and exercises provided are tools to empower you, but the true magic lies within your willingness to embark on this profound journey of self-trust.

Are you ready to take the first step, to cast aside the cloak of doubt and uncertainty, and to embrace the boundless potential that resides within you? If so, let us begin this odyssey towards self-trust, authenticity, and a fully lived life- your way.

# CHAPTER 1

## THE IMPORTANCE OF SELF-TRUST

"As soon as you trust yourself, you will know how to live."

—— **Johann Wolfgang von Goethe**

# THE IMPORTANCE OF SELF-TRUST

- Defining Self-Trust

- Why Self-Trust Matters

- The Consequences of Self-Doubt

## Defining Self-Trust

Self-trust, often referred to as self-belief or self-confidence, is the fundamental belief in your own abilities, judgments, and decisions. It's your unwavering faith in yourself to navigate life's challenges, make choices that align with your values, and pursue your goals and dreams. This inner trust is the foundation upon which your self-esteem, self-worth, and overall well-being are built.

Self-trust is not a static attribute but a dynamic and evolving quality. It can be strengthened, nurtured, or, in some cases, eroded over time. It encompasses several key elements:

1. **Trust in Your Abilities:** This involves having confidence in your skills, talents, and competencies. It's the belief that you can learn, adapt, and overcome obstacles as they arise.

2. **Trust in Your Judgment:** Self-trust extends to your capacity to make sound decisions based on your values, intuition, and experiences. It's about relying on your inner wisdom to guide you.

3. **Trust in Your Authenticity:** Embracing your authentic self is integral to self-trust. It means being true to your values, beliefs, and desires rather than trying to conform to external expectations.

4. **Trust in Your Resilience:** Self-trust includes believing you can bounce back from setbacks and failures. It's the understanding that adversity is a part of life but doesn't define your worth or potential.

## Why Self-Trust Matters

Self-trust is not a luxury; it's a necessity for leading a fulfilling and meaningful life. Here's why it matters:

1. Empowerment and Autonomy:

Self-trust empowers you to take control of your life. It allows you to make decisions independently and take ownership of the consequences, whether they are positive or negative. When you trust yourself, you are less reliant on external validation and more in tune with your inner compass.

2. Resilience in the Face of Challenges:

Life is filled with ups and downs, and self-trust is your shield against adversity. When you trust your abilities and judgment, you're more likely to face challenges with confidence and resilience. Failures and setbacks become opportunities for growth rather than sources of despair.

3. Authenticity and Fulfillment:

Self-trust encourages you to embrace your true self. It enables you to pursue your passions, values, and dreams, leading to a life that aligns with your authentic desires. Living authentically is a crucial ingredient for long-term happiness and fulfillment.

4. Better Relationships:

Self-trust can positively impact your relationships with others. When you trust yourself, you're more likely to establish healthy boundaries, communicate effectively, and make choices in the best interest of you and those you care about.

5. Confidence and Self-Esteem:

Self-trust is a cornerstone of self-confidence and healthy self-esteem. Believing in your abilities and worth is essential for setting and achieving personal or professional goals.

## The Consequences of Self-Doubt

On the flip side, when self-trust is lacking, self-doubt takes its place, and this can have detrimental effects on various aspects of your life:

1. Inaction and Procrastination:

Self-doubt can lead to paralysis. When you second-guess yourself at every turn, you may hesitate to take action, hindering personal and professional growth.

2. Fear of Failure:

Self-doubt often intensifies the fear of failure. This fear can be paralyzing, preventing you from pursuing your dreams or taking calculated risks that could lead to success.

3. Poor Decision-Making:

When you doubt your judgment, you may become overly influenced by the opinions and advice of others. This can result in decisions that don't align with your values or desires.

## 4. Negative Self-Talk:

Self-doubt often manifests as a harsh inner critic. You may constantly berate yourself, undermining your self-esteem and self-worth.

## 5. Relationship Struggles:

Self-doubt can spill over into your relationships, causing you to doubt the intentions and feelings of others. This can lead to insecurity, jealousy, and strained connections.

## 6. Lack of Fulfillment:

Ultimately, self-doubt can prevent you from living authentically and pursuing your passions. It can keep you trapped in a cycle of conformity and unfulfilling choices.

Understanding the importance of self-trust and the consequences of self-doubt is the first step on your journey to learning to trust yourself. In the following chapters, we will explore strategies and techniques to cultivate self-trust, nurture self-belief, and break free from self-doubt, ultimately empowering you to lead a more authentic and fulfilling life.

### *From Self-Doubt to Self-Trust: A Journey of Transformation*

A woman named Sarah lived in a quiet suburban neighborhood, nestled among the neatly trimmed lawns and white picket fences. On the surface, her life seemed perfect. She had a loving family, a secure job, and a circle of friends who admired her poise and competence. Yet, beneath the facade, Sarah grappled with a persistent self-doubt.

## Defining Self-Trust

Sarah's self-doubt had its roots in her childhood. Growing up, she often heard critical remarks from her parents, who had high expectations for her academic and personal achievements. As a result, she developed an inner critic that constantly questioned her abilities and worth. This critical voice had been with her for so long that she accepted it as a part of her identity.

One evening, while attending a self-help workshop, Sarah had an epiphany. She realized that self-trust meant challenging that inner critic and redefining her relationship with herself. It wasn't about ignoring her flaws but recognizing her strengths and abilities. Sarah decided to embark on a journey of self-discovery and self-trust.

## Why Self-Trust Matters

Sarah understood that self-trust was crucial for her well-being and personal growth. She had seen how her self-doubt had held her back from pursuing her dreams and embracing her authenticity. It was time for a change.

As Sarah began her journey, she discovered that self-trust brought empowerment and autonomy. She started to make choices aligned with her true desires, regardless of external expectations. She enrolled in an art class, a passion she had suppressed for years, and found immense joy in creating.

Self-trust also helped Sarah face life's challenges with resilience. When her job became more demanding, instead of doubting her abilities, she believed in her capacity to adapt and learn. Failures and setbacks no longer crushed her spirit; they became stepping stones toward personal growth.

**The Consequences of Self-Doubt**

Sarah had experienced firsthand the consequences of self-doubt. In the past, she had often procrastinated on projects out of fear that they wouldn't meet her high standards. This had stalled her career progression and hindered her personal development.

Her relationships, too, bore the weight of her self-doubt. Sarah constantly sought validation from others, which strained her friendships and marriage. She realized that until she trusted herself, it would be easier to establish healthy boundaries and communicate effectively.

The most significant change Sarah noticed was in her own self-esteem and self-worth. As she began to trust herself more, the negative self-talk that had haunted her for years started to quiet down. She realized that she deserved love and respect just as she was, flaws and all.

Sarah's journey from self-doubt to self-trust was not linear or without challenges. It involved deep introspection, self-compassion, and a therapist's and close friends' support. But over time, her self-belief grew stronger, and her inner critic's voice grew fainter.

In the end, Sarah's transformation was a testament to the importance of self-trust. She learned it wasn't about becoming perfect but accepting her imperfections and trusting herself to navigate life's uncertainties. Her newfound self-trust allowed her to live authentically, pursue her passions, and nurture deeper and more fulfilling relationships.

Sarah's story serves as an inspiring reminder that the journey of self-trust is one well worth taking, for it can lead to a life filled with confidence, resilience, and an unwavering belief in one's own abilities and worth.

— • —

# CHAPTER 2

## UNDERSTANDING SELF-DOUBT

"Trust thyself: every heart vibrates to that iron string."

—— **Ralph Waldo Emmerson**

—•—

# UNDERSTANDING SELF-DOUBT

- The Origins of Self-Doubt

- The Inner Critic

- How Self-Doubt Holds You Back

## The Origins of Self-Doubt

Self-doubt is a complex and deeply ingrained emotion that can trace its roots to various sources. Understanding where self-doubt originates is the first step in overcoming it.

## 1. Early Childhood Experiences:

Often, self-doubt finds its beginnings in childhood. Negative experiences, criticism, or unrealistic expectations from parents, teachers, or peers can seed doubt. For example, if a child is repeatedly told they're not good enough or that their efforts are inadequate, these messages can become internalized, creating a persistent sense of inadequacy.

## 2. Comparison to Others:

In today's interconnected world, the constant comparison to others, fueled by social media and societal pressures, can foster self-doubt. Seeing others' seemingly flawless lives and achievements can make individuals question their own worth and accomplishments.

## 3. Traumatic Events:

Traumatic events such as failure, rejection, or loss can trigger self-doubt. These experiences can create a fear of repeating the same mistakes or facing similar pain, leading to hesitation and self-questioning.

## 4. Cultural and Societal Expectations:

Cultural norms and societal expectations can play a significant role in fostering self-doubt. Unrealistic beauty standards, gender roles, and success benchmarks imposed by society can lead individuals to question their abilities and self-worth.

## 5. Perfectionism:

Perfectionism, the relentless pursuit of flawlessness, often goes hand in hand with self-doubt. The constant need to meet impossibly high standards can generate feelings of inadequacy when those standards aren't met.

## The Inner Critic

At the heart of self-doubt lies the inner critic, a relentless voice that consistently undermines self-confidence. The inner critic exaggerates flaws, magnifies mistakes, and diminishes achievements. Recognizing and understanding the inner critic is crucial for addressing self-doubt.

## 1. Identifying Your Inner Critic:

Your inner critic often operates on autopilot, making it challenging to recognize. Start by paying attention to the negative self-talk in your mind. What does this voice say when you make a mistake or face a challenge?

## 2. Understanding Its Origin:

Your inner critic's origin can often be traced back to the critical voices of authority figures from your past or the internalization of societal expectations. Understanding where this voice comes from can help you separate it from your true self.

## 3. Challenging the Inner Critic:

Challenge your inner critic's assumptions and distortions. Ask yourself if the criticism is based on facts or irrational beliefs. What evidence supports or contradicts these negative thoughts?

## 4. Cultivating Self-Compassion:

Self-compassion, as explored in Chapter 4, involves treating yourself with kindness and understanding, especially in times of failure or self-doubt. Developing self-compassion can help quiet the inner critic's harsh judgments.

## How Self-Doubt Holds You Back

Self-doubt can have far-reaching consequences, hindering personal and professional growth in numerous ways:

## 1. Procrastination and Inaction:

When plagued by self-doubt, individuals may hesitate to take action or delay pursuing their goals out of fear of failure. This procrastination can hinder progress and keep them stuck in a cycle of inaction.

## 2. Fear of Failure:

Self-doubt often intensifies the fear of failure. This fear can be paralyzing, preventing individuals from taking calculated risks or trying new things, which are essential for personal development.

### 3. Impostor Syndrome:

Impostor syndrome, a specific manifestation of self-doubt, makes individuals believe that their achievements result from luck rather than their abilities. This can lead to feelings of fraudulence and prevent them from acknowledging their accomplishments.

### 4. Underachievement:

Self-doubt can limit individuals' belief in their capabilities, leading to underachievement. They may settle for mediocrity or avoid challenges that could lead to growth and success.

### 5. Strained Relationships:

Self-doubt can negatively impact relationships by creating insecurity, jealousy, and a constant need for validation. It can hinder effective communication and the establishment of healthy boundaries.

Understanding the origins of self-doubt, recognizing the inner critic, and acknowledging how self-doubt holds you back are crucial steps to self-trust. In the following chapters, we will delve deeper into strategies and techniques to challenge self-doubt, cultivate self-compassion, and ultimately build the foundation of self-trust needed for a more fulfilling and empowered life.*B reaking the Chains of Self-Doubt: A Personal Journey*

Julia sat in her small, cluttered office, staring at her desk's stack of unfinished projects. Despite her impeccable academic record and years of experience in her field, she was overwhelmed by self-doubt.

## The Origins of Self-Doubt

Julia's self-doubt could be traced back to her childhood. Growing up, she was always the "good girl" who aimed to please her parents. Her father, in particular, had exceptionally high expectations for her academic performance. While he meant well, his constant insistence on perfection instilled in Julia a fear of failure and an unrelenting drive to meet unrealistic standards.

Throughout her school years, Julia excelled academically. She was the valedictorian of her high school class and graduated with top honors from a prestigious university. However, her achievements came at a price. She felt immense pressure to maintain her perfect track record and constantly questioned whether she was truly as capable as her grades suggested.

## The Inner Critic

Julia's inner critic was a constant companion throughout her life. It was a voice that whispered in her ear, telling her that she wasn't good enough, that she was bound to make a mistake sooner or later, and that others would eventually see through her façade of competence.

This inner critic's influence extended far beyond her professional life. It affected her personal relationships as well. Julia was always seeking approval and validation from others, unable to fully accept herself for who she was. Her self-doubt had manifested as a need for external reassurance and a fear of rejection.

## How Self-Doubt Holds You Back

Julia's self-doubt had tangible consequences in her life. It wasn't just a nagging feeling; it was a force that held her back in various ways.

### 1. Procrastination and Inaction:

Julia often found herself procrastinating on essential projects. She would delay making decisions and taking action out of fear that her choices might lead to failure or criticism. This procrastination hindered her career progression.

### 2. Fear of Failure:

The fear of failure was a constant presence in Julia's life. She avoided challenges that might test her abilities, choosing the familiar and safe over the unknown. As a result, she missed out on opportunities for growth and advancement.

## 3. Impostor Syndrome:

Julia suffered from a severe case of impostor syndrome. Despite her impressive academic and professional achievements, she believed that she didn't deserve her success. She was convinced she was merely lucky and would eventually be exposed as a fraud.

## 4. Strained Relationships:

Julia's self-doubt affected her relationships. She was often overly sensitive to criticism and had difficulty accepting compliments. Her constant need for validation strained her friendships and made it challenging to form deep connections.

## Breaking Free from Self-Doubt

Recognizing the origins of her self-doubt and the role of her inner critic was a turning point for Julia. She realized that her father's well-intentioned pressure had shaped her self-image and hindered her self-trust. She embarked on a journey of self-discovery and self-compassion to break free from the chains of self-doubt.

Through therapy and self-help books, Julia learned to challenge her inner critic's harsh judgments. She practiced self-compassion and began to acknowledge her achievements without downplaying them. Over time, she started to believe in her own abilities and values, independent of external validation.

As her self-trust grew, Julia felt more empowered to take risks in her career and personal life. She no longer allowed fear of failure to paralyze her. Instead, she viewed mistakes as opportunities for learning and growth.

Julia's story is a testament to the power of understanding self-doubt, confronting the inner critic, and breaking free from the limitations it imposes. Her journey inspires anyone wrestling with self-doubt, showing that self-awareness and self-compassion can overcome the most deeply ingrained doubts and build a foundation of self-trust for a brighter future.

— ⁛ —

# CHAPTER 3

## BUILDING SELF-AWARENESS

"*I* care for myself. The more solitary, the more friendless, the more unsustained I am, the more I will respect myself."

—— **Charlotte Brontë**

—·—

— • —

# Building Self-Awareness

- The Power of Self-Reflection

- Recognizing Your Strengths and Weaknesses

- Embracing Your Uniqueness

## The Power of Self-Reflection

Self-awareness is the cornerstone of personal growth and the first step in building self-trust. It involves a deep and honest understanding of oneself, including thoughts, feelings, values, and behaviors. Self-awareness is like holding a mirror to your inner self, allowing you to see who you are.

## 1. The Practice of Self-Reflection:

Self-awareness begins with self-reflection. It's taking time to introspect, ask meaningful questions, and examine your thoughts and actions without judgment. Journaling, meditation, or simply quiet contemplation can be practical tools for self-reflection.

## 2. Understanding Your Motivations:

Self-reflection helps you uncover the motivations behind your actions. Why do you make certain choices? What drives your desires and goals? Understanding these motivations can reveal your core values and desires.

## 3. Recognizing Patterns:

Self-awareness allows you to identify recurring patterns in your thoughts and behaviors. These patterns may be constructive or self-limiting; recognizing them is essential for personal growth.

## 4. Embracing Vulnerability:

Self-reflection may uncover vulnerabilities and insecurities. Embracing these aspects of yourself without judgment is a crucial part of self-awareness. Through vulnerability, you can build a more authentic and trusting relationship with yourself.

## Recognizing Your Strengths and Weaknesses

Understanding your strengths and weaknesses is a key component of self-awareness. It's about acknowledging your areas of competence and areas where you need improvement.

## 1. Identifying Your Strengths:

Take inventory of your strengths. What are you naturally good at? What skills have you developed over time? Recognizing your strengths can boost your self-esteem and confidence.

## 2. Embracing Your Weaknesses:

Self-awareness also means accepting your weaknesses. We all have areas where we struggle or make mistakes. Instead of viewing weaknesses as failures, see them as opportunities for growth. You can become a more well-rounded individual by acknowledging and addressing weaknesses.

## 3. Seeking Feedback:

Don't hesitate to seek feedback from others. Trusted friends, family members, or mentors can provide valuable insights into your strengths and weaknesses that you might not see in yourself. Be open to constructive criticism.

## Embracing Your Uniqueness

Each person is a unique combination of experiences, talents, and perspectives. Embracing your uniqueness is a vital aspect of self-awareness and self-trust.

## 1. Celebrating Your Uniqueness:

Embrace the fact that you are unlike anyone else. Celebrate your individuality, quirks, and idiosyncrasies. Your uniqueness is what makes you unique and valuable.

## 2. Authenticity Over Conformity:

Self-awareness encourages you to be authentic rather than conform to societal expectations or pressures. When you align your actions and choices with your true self, you build a more profound sense of self-trust.

## 3. Fostering Self-Compassion:

Embracing your uniqueness requires self-compassion. Be kind to yourself, especially when you encounter challenges or setbacks. Remember that it's okay to be imperfect; no one is flawless.

## The Journey of Self-Awareness

Building self-awareness is not a one-time event but an ongoing journey. It involves continuous self-reflection, a willingness to learn, and an openness to change. The more you understand yourself—your motivations, strengths, weaknesses, and uniqueness—the more you can develop a strong foundation of self-trust.

In the chapters, we will explore how self-awareness contributes to building self-trust and provide practical exercises and strategies to enhance your self-awareness. Remember that this journey is not about perfection but about self-acceptance and growth.

### *Unveiling the True Self: A Journey of Self-Awareness*

Maria found herself at a crossroads in life. She had always been driven, excelling academically and professionally, but she felt a deep sense of emptiness and self-doubt that she couldn't ignore any longer. It was time for her to embark on a journey of self-discovery and self-awareness.

### The Power of Self-Reflection

Maria's journey began with self-reflection. She realized she had been so focused on achieving external success that she had neglected her inner world. The constant hustle had left her feeling disconnected from her true self.

### 1. Journaling as a Path to Self-Reflection:

Maria started journaling regularly. She would set aside time each day to reflect on her thoughts, emotions, and experiences. This practice allowed her to gain insights into her inner world and uncover long-buried feelings and desires.

## 2. Discovering Core Values:

Through self-reflection, Maria identified her core values—authenticity, creativity, and connection. She realized that she had been living in a way that didn't align with these values, contributing to her sense of emptiness.

## Recognizing Your Strengths and Weaknesses

Maria's journey toward self-awareness also involved recognizing her strengths and weaknesses. She had always been driven to excel, but she had never taken the time to acknowledge her innate talents and areas where she needed growth.

## 1. Identifying Strengths:

Maria sought feedback from friends and colleagues. She was pleasantly surprised to discover that those who knew her well highly regarded her empathetic nature, problem-solving skills, and ability to connect with others.

## 2. Embracing Weaknesses:

Maria tended to be overly critical of herself. Through self-awareness, she learned to embrace her imperfections and see her weaknesses as opportunities for growth. She sought professional development in areas where she felt less confident, viewing them as chances to learn and improve.

## Embracing Your Uniqueness

As Maria delved deeper into her self-awareness journey, she learned to embrace her uniqueness. She realized she didn't have to conform to societal expectations or fit into a predefined mold to be happy.

### 1. Celebrating Authenticity:

Maria decided to live authentically, even if it meant making unconventional choices. She pursued creative interests that had long been neglected, such as painting and writing, and found immense joy in expressing her true self.

### 2. Self-Compassion as a Guiding Light:

Embracing her uniqueness also required self-compassion. Maria learned to be kind and forgiving to herself, especially when she faced setbacks or made mistakes along the way. This self-compassion allowed her to navigate the ups and downs of her journey with resilience.

## The Transformation

Over time, Maria's journey of self-awareness transformed her life. She let go of the need for external validation and began trusting her own judgment. As she embraced her authenticity, she found that her relationships deepened, and she attracted people who appreciated her for who she indeed was.

Maria's career took an unexpected turn as she pursued her creative passions, ultimately finding fulfillment in a job aligned with her core values. She had discovered her strengths, acknowledged her weaknesses, and fully embraced her uniqueness.

Her journey was not without challenges, and there were moments when self-doubt resurfaced. However, Maria's newfound self-awareness was a guiding light, allowing her to recognize those moments and respond with self-compassion and self-trust.

Maria's story illustrates the transformative power of self-awareness. It's a reminder that the path to self-discovery is a continuous journey that can lead to a deeper connection with oneself and a more authentic and fulfilling life.

——— ∘ ———

# CHAPTER 4

## CULTIVATING SELF-COMPASSION

"The greatest thing in the world is to know
how to belong to oneself."

—— **Michel de Montaigne**

———— ❖ ————

## CULTIVATING SELF-COMPASSION

- The Role of Self-Compassion in Self-Trust

- Practicing Self-Kindness

- Overcoming Self-Criticism

### The Role of Self-Compassion in Self-Trust

Self-compassion is extending the same kindness, understanding, and support to yourself that you would offer to a dear friend facing a challenging situation. It plays a pivotal role in building self-trust, bridging self-awareness and self-belief.

### 1. The Inner Dialogue:

Self-compassion transforms your inner dialogue from one of self-criticism and judgment to one of self-kindness and empathy. Instead of criticizing yourself for mistakes or perceived shortcomings, you offer yourself the same comfort and reassurance that you would to a friend.

## 2. Self-Acceptance:

Self-compassion fosters self-acceptance, allowing you to embrace your flaws, vulnerabilities, and imperfections as part of your humanity. It's an acknowledgment that no one is perfect, and self-worth is not contingent on being flawless.

## 3. Resilience in the Face of Challenges:

When you practice self-compassion, you build resilience. You are better equipped to handle setbacks and failures by approaching them with self-kindness and believing in your ability to learn and grow.

## Practicing Self-Kindness

Cultivating self-compassion begins with practicing self-kindness. It's about treating yourself with the same warmth and care you would extend to a loved one.

## 1. Self-Love and Self-Care:

Make self-love and self-care a priority in your life. Treat yourself with the same consideration that you give to others. This might involve relaxing, pursuing hobbies, or simply resting when needed.

## 2. Embracing Mistakes:

Instead of viewing mistakes as failures, see them as opportunities for growth. When you make a mistake, treat yourself with understanding and patience. Ask yourself what you can learn from the experience.

## 3. Self-Validation:

Practice self-validation by acknowledging your accomplishments and celebrating your successes, no matter how small. Be sure to affirm your worth before external validation.

## 4. Self-Encouragement:

Be your own cheerleader. When facing challenges or pursuing goals, offer yourself words of encouragement and motivation. Remind yourself of your strengths and your capacity to overcome obstacles.

## Overcoming Self-Criticism

Overcoming self-criticism is an integral part of cultivating self-compassion. It involves challenging the negative self-talk that undermines self-trust.

## 1. Awareness of Self-Criticism:

The first step in overcoming self-criticism is becoming aware of it. Pay attention to the negative thoughts and self-judgments that arise in your mind. Recognize when your inner critic is at work.

## 2. Questioning the Validity:

Challenge the validity of self-critical thoughts. Are they based on evidence, or are they irrational beliefs? Often, self-criticism exaggerates flaws and minimizes strengths.

## 3. Reframing Self-Criticism:

Reframe self-criticism into constructive self-feedback. Instead of saying, "I'm a failure," try, "I made a mistake, and I can learn from it." This shift in perspective promotes self-compassion.

## 4. Mindfulness and Self-Compassion Practices:

Engage in mindfulness and self-compassion practices, such as loving-kindness meditation or self-compassion exercises. These techniques can help you develop a more compassionate and nurturing relationship with yourself.

## The Transformational Power of Self-Compassion

Cultivating self-compassion is a transformative journey that can lead to a profound sense of self-trust and self-belief. It allows you to be more resilient in the face of challenges, more accepting of your flaws, and more compassionate toward yourself in times of difficulty.

Self-compassion is not a sign of weakness; it's a strength that empowers you to embrace your authentic self and build a foundation of self-trust that can withstand the trials and tribulations of life. In the following chapters, we will explore how self-compassion can be integrated into your daily life through practical exercises and strategies, enabling you to nurture a deeper and more loving relationship with yourself.

### *Rising from Self-Critique to Self-Compassion: A Journey of Transformation*

Mark was trapped in a relentless cycle of self-criticism in a bustling city. He had always been ambitious, setting high standards for himself in both his career and personal life. However, his inner critic had grown louder over the years, eroding his self-trust and causing a persistent sense of inadequacy.

### The Role of Self-Compassion in Self-Trust

Mark's journey toward self-compassion began with a deep realization: the more he criticized himself, the less he trusted his abilities. He understood that self-compassion was not a sign of weakness but a source of inner strength and resilience.

### 1. Transforming Self-Talk:

Mark started to change his inner dialogue. Instead of berating himself for every mistake or perceived shortcoming, he practiced self-kindness. He offered himself words of encouragement and understanding, much like he would to a close friend.

## 2. Embracing Vulnerability:

Mark acknowledged his vulnerabilities and accepted them as part of his humanity. He understood that nobody was flawless, and his self-worth was not contingent on perfection.

## 3. Building Resilience:

Self-compassion gave Mark the resilience to face challenges and setbacks with grace. He approached difficulties as opportunities for growth, knowing that he could learn from them and emerge stronger.

## Practicing Self-Kindness

Self-kindness became a cornerstone of Mark's journey toward self-compassion. He gradually incorporated self-love and self-care into his daily life.

## 1. Prioritizing Self-Care:

Mark made self-care a priority. He dedicated time to activities that brought him joy and relaxation, such as taking long walks in nature, reading, and practicing mindfulness meditation.

## 2. Embracing Imperfection:

Instead of striving for perfection, Mark embraced his imperfections. He recognized that his perceived flaws were part of his uniqueness and contributed to his growth.

## 3. Self-Celebration:

Mark learned to celebrate his successes, no matter how small. He acknowledged his accomplishments and validated his worth rather than seeking external validation.

## Overcoming Self-Criticism

Overcoming self-criticism was another crucial aspect of Mark's journey. He took deliberate steps to challenge and reframe his self-critical thoughts.

## 1. Awareness of Self-Criticism:

Mark became vigilant about his self-critical thoughts. He learned to recognize when his inner critic was most vocal, particularly during moments of failure or self-doubt.

## 2. Challenging Negative Thoughts:

Mark questioned the validity of self-criticism. He asked himself if these thoughts were based on facts or irrational beliefs. Often, he realized that his self-criticism was exaggerated and unhelpful.

## 3. Reframing Criticism into Self-Feedback:

Mark reframed self-criticism into constructive self-feedback. Instead of saying, "I'm a failure," he shifted his perspective to, "I made a mistake, and I can learn from it." This subtle language change promoted self-compassion.

## The Transformation

As Mark continued his journey toward self-compassion, he experienced a profound transformation. His self-trust grew stronger, and he began to believe in his abilities and worth. Self-doubt no longer held him back; it had been replaced by self-belief.

Mark's career benefited as well. With self-compassion as his guide, he was better equipped to navigate challenges and setbacks. His resilience and self-assurance allowed him to take calculated risks and achieve professional success he had never thought possible.

But the most significant transformation was in Mark's relationship with himself. He transitioned from being his harshest critic to his greatest supporter and ally. His journey from self-critique to self-compassion restored his self-trust and opened the door to a life filled with authenticity, self-acceptance, and profound self-belief.

Mark's story is a powerful reminder of the transformative potential of self-compassion. It's a testament to the fact that
self-kindness and self-acceptance are the keys to breaking free
from the chains of self-criticism and nurturing a deep sense of
self-trust.

— ❖ —

# CHAPTER 5

## SETTING AUTHENTIC GOALS

"In yourself right now is all the place you've got."

—— **Flannery O'Connor**

—  •  —

# SETTING AUTHENTIC GOALS

- The Difference Between Authentic and External Goals

- Aligning Your Goals with Your Values

- Taking Steps Toward Your Authentic Self

## The Difference Between Authentic and External Goals

Setting goals is a fundamental aspect of personal growth and self-trust. However, not all goals are created equal. External influences drive some, while others emerge from your authentic self. Understanding the difference between these types of goals is essential in building self-trust.

### 1. External Goals:

Societal pressures, family expectations, or the desire for external validation often shape external goals. These goals are usually centered around achieving status, wealth, or recognition. Pursuing external goals may lead to short-term success but often leaves individuals feeling fulfilled.

## 2. Authentic Goals:

Authentic goals, on the other hand, are aligned with your actual values, interests, and passions. They reflect your unique identity and are deeply meaningful to you. Pursuing authentic goals brings a sense of purpose and fulfillment that transcends external validation.

## Aligning Your Goals with Your Values

To set authentic goals, aligning them with your core values is crucial. Your values are the principles that guide your life and shape your decisions. When your goals align with your values, you are more likely to feel a sense of purpose and fulfillment in your pursuits.

## 1. Identifying Your Core Values:

Take time to identify your core values. What principles are most important to you in life? Some typical values include integrity, creativity, compassion, and authenticity. Your values are unique to you and may evolve over time.

## 2. Setting Value-Based Goals:

Once you clearly understand your values, set goals that reflect them. For example, if creativity is a core value, consider setting a goal to pursue a creative hobby or career path. Value-based goals are more likely to resonate with your authentic self.

### 3. Evaluating Existing Goals:

If you have existing goals that don't align with your values, evaluate whether they are worth pursuing. Sometimes, it's necessary to let go of goals that no longer serve your authentic self to make room for those that do.

### Taking Steps Toward Your Authentic Self

Setting and pursuing authentic goals is not just about achieving external success; it's a journey of self-discovery and self-trust. Here are steps to help you take action and align your goals with your authentic self.

### 1. Self-Reflection:

Engage in self-reflection to clarify who you are and what truly matters to you. Consider your strengths, passions, and what brings you joy.

### 2. Define Your Authentic Goals:

Define clear and specific authentic goals. Break them down into smaller, achievable steps. Ensure that each goal resonates with your values and represents your authentic self.

## 3. Take Action:

Take deliberate steps toward your goals. Consistent action, even small ones, can lead to significant progress. Embrace challenges and setbacks as part of the journey.

## 4. Stay True to Yourself:

Along the way, stay true to your authentic self. Avoid compromising your values or authenticity for external validation or success.

## 5. Embrace Growth and Adaptation:

Recognize that your authentic self is not static. It grows and evolves with time and experience. Embrace change and adapt your goals accordingly as you discover more about yourself.

## Authentic Goals and Self-Trust

Setting and pursuing authentic goals is a powerful way to build self-trust. When your goals align with your true self and values, you develop a sense of integrity and authenticity. You become more confident in making decisions and navigating life's challenges because you trust yourself to make choices that honor your authenticity.

In the chapters ahead, we will delve deeper into the practical aspects of goal setting and provide exercises and strategies to help you identify and pursue authentic goals. Remember that your authentic self is your greatest asset, and setting authentic goals is the path to unlocking your fullest potential and living a life that resonates with your deepest values and desires.

### *Chasing Authenticity: A Journey of Self-Discovery*

Leslie was leading a life that many would envy. She had a high-paying job, a luxurious apartment, and a thriving social circle. Yet, despite her external success, Leslie felt an inexplicable emptiness. She realized that her goals were not aligned with her true self.

### The Difference Between Authentic and External Goals

Leslie's journey toward authentic goals began with a profound realization: she had been chasing external goals that did not resonate with her authentic self. Her aspirations were shaped by societal expectations and the desire for recognition, leaving her feeling unfulfilled.

### 1. External Goals:

Leslie's external goals had been driven by societal pressures and her family's expectations. She had pursued a career in finance because it was considered prestigious and financially rewarding, not because it aligned with her passions or values.

## 2. Authentic Goals:

Leslie started to explore her authentic goals. She recognized that her true passions lay in art and community service. She felt a deep sense of purpose and fulfillment in these areas, far beyond what her external goals had provided.

## Aligning Your Goals with Your Values

To set authentic goals, Leslie knew she had to align them with her core values. Her values were the compass guiding her toward a more meaningful life.

## 1. Identifying Core Values:

Leslie embarked on a journey of self-discovery to identify her core values. Through journaling and introspection, she realized that creativity, compassion, and community were at the heart of who she was.

## 2. Setting Value-Based Goals:

With a clearer understanding of her values, Leslie began setting value-based goals. She enrolled in art classes and volunteered at a local shelter, aligning her pursuits with her authentic self.

## 3. Evaluating Existing Goals:

Leslie assessed her financial goals and realized they no longer resonated with her authentic self. It wasn't easy, but she transitioned away from her finance career and toward her newfound passion for art and community service.

## Taking Steps Toward Your Authentic Self

Leslie's journey toward authentic goals was not without challenges but a path of self-discovery and self-trust.

## 1. Self-Reflection:

Leslie engaged in self-reflection, seeking to understand her strengths, passions, and what brought her joy. She uncovered a love for painting and a deep desire to impact her community positively.

## 2. Defining Authentic Goals:

Leslie defined clear and specific authentic goals. She aimed to become a professional artist and use her art to raise awareness and funds for charitable causes.

## 3. Taking Action:

Leslie took deliberate steps toward her authentic goals. She enrolled in art classes, exhibited her work, and participated in community service projects. Each action brought her closer to her authentic self.

## 4. Staying True to Herself:

Along the way, Leslie remained true to her authentic self. She resisted the temptation to measure her worth by external success metrics and instead focused on the fulfillment she found in her pursuits.

## 5. Embracing Growth and Adaptation:

Leslie embraced personal growth and adaptation. Her journey was not linear, but she recognized that her authentic self was evolving, and her goals adjusted accordingly.

## Authentic Goals and Self-Trust

Setting and pursuing authentic goals transformed Leslie's life. Her sense of self-trust grew stronger as she aligned her goals with her true self and values. She became more confident in her decisions and resilient in facing challenges.

Leslie's career in art and community service flourished. Her art exhibitions raised funds for local charities, and she found deep fulfillment in positively impacting her community. Most importantly, she felt a profound sense of authenticity and self-trust that she had never experienced.

Leslie's story is a testament to the transformative power of aligning goals with one's authentic self. It underscores the importance of pursuing passions and values, rather than external expectations, as the key to building self-trust and living a fulfilling life that resonates with one's deepest desires.

# CHAPTER 6

## EMBRACING FAILURE AND RESILIENCE

"What the mind can conceive and believe
and the heart desire, you can achieve."

—— **Norman Vincent Peale**

—·—

## Embracing Failure and Resilience

- The Fear of Failure

- Learning from Mistakes

- Building Resilience Through Adversity

### The Fear of Failure

Fear of failure is a universal human experience. It's the apprehension, anxiety, or dread associated with the possibility of falling short of our goals or expectations. This fear can paralyze us from taking risks and pursuing our dreams. However, it's essential to understand that failure is an inevitable part of life, and embracing it is crucial for building self-trust.

### 1. The Paralyzing Effect of Fear:

The fear of failure often keeps us stuck in our comfort zones, afraid to step into the unknown. We avoid taking risks, even when those risks could lead to growth and personal development.

## 2. Perfectionism and Fear:

Perfectionism is closely linked to the fear of failure. The relentless pursuit of perfection sets unrealistic standards and makes us highly susceptible to self-doubt and criticism.

## 3. External Validation and Fear:

Seeking external validation intensifies the fear of failure. When our self-worth is tied to the approval of others, we become afraid of making mistakes that might lead to rejection or criticism.

## Learning from Mistakes

Embracing failure doesn't mean celebrating it or seeking it out, but rather recognizing that it's an integral part of the learning process. When viewed through the lens of growth and self-improvement, mistakes can be powerful teachers.

## 1. The Wisdom of Mistakes:

Mistakes offer valuable lessons and insights. They provide an opportunity to learn, adapt, and develop new skills. Without errors, there can be no growth.

## 2. Reframing Failure:

Rather than seeing failure as an endpoint, view it as a stepping stone to success. Every setback brings you one step closer to achieving your goals.

### 3. Self-Compassion and Mistakes:

Practicing self-compassion when you make mistakes is essential. Instead of berating yourself, treat yourself with kindness and understanding. Remember that everyone makes mistakes; it's part of being human.

### Building Resilience Through Adversity

Resilience is the ability to bounce back from adversity, setbacks, and challenges. It's a vital trait for building self-trust because it empowers us to persevere in facing difficulties.

### 1. Adversity as an Opportunity:

Adversity is not the enemy; it's an opportunity for growth. Resilience allows us to navigate adversity with courage and grace.

### 2. Developing Resilience:

Resilience can be developed over time. It involves cultivating a growth mindset, maintaining a support system, and practicing self-care.

### 3. Learning from Setbacks:

Resilience enables us to learn from setbacks rather than be defeated by them. We become more adaptable and better equipped to handle future challenges.

## The Power of Vulnerability

Vulnerability is often associated with weakness, but it's a source of strength. Embracing vulnerability means acknowledging our imperfections and being open to taking risks.

## 1. Vulnerability and Authenticity:

Vulnerability is closely connected to authenticity. When we allow ourselves to be vulnerable, we become more authentic and connect with others deeper.

## 2. Vulnerability and Self-Trust:

Embracing vulnerability is a powerful way to build self-trust. It involves trusting yourself to handle the outcomes of taking risks, whether they lead to success or failure.

## The Resilient Path to Self-Trust

Embracing failure and building resilience is a transformative journey. It's a shift from fearing loss to seeing it as a natural part of life and personal growth. It's about recognizing that setbacks are not the end of the road but stepping stones on your path to self-trust.

In the following chapters, we will explore practical strategies for facing failure with resilience, embracing vulnerability, and using setbacks as opportunities for personal growth. Remember that self-trust is not about never failing; it's about having the confidence to rise stronger each time life presents you with challenges.

## *Rising Strong: A Story of Embracing Failure and Building Resilience*

Emily embarked on a journey to transform her relationship with failure and resilience. Emily had always been cautious, preferring to stay within her comfort zone to avoid the fear of failure. But life had other plans for her.

## The Fear of Failure

Emily's fear of failure was deeply ingrained. As a child, she was praised for her academic achievements and had been taught that success equated to high grades and accolades. This early conditioning led to a paralyzing fear of making mistakes or falling short of expectations.

## 1. The Academic Pressure:

Emily excelled in school, but the pressure to maintain her performance weighed heavily on her. She internalized the belief that anything less than perfection was unacceptable.

## 2. Perfectionism Takes Hold:

This fear of failure evolved into perfectionism. Emily set impossibly high standards for herself in all aspects of life, from her career to her relationships.

## 3. Seeking External Validation:

Emily's self-worth became tied to external validation. She constantly sought approval and praise from others, fearing that her intrinsic value was contingent on their opinions.

## Learning from Mistakes

Emily's journey toward embracing failure began when she decided to take up a new hobby—painting. At first, she approached painting with trepidation, fearing that she would not be good enough. She soon realized that making mistakes was integral to the creative process.

## 1. The Wisdom of Mistakes:

With each stroke of the brush, Emily made mistakes. But she learned that these mistakes were not failures but opportunities to experiment, learn, and grow as an artist.

## 2. Reframing Failure:

Emily reframed her view of failure. She started seeing it as a necessary step on the path to improvement. Every smudged canvas and misplaced color became a lesson in resilience and adaptability.

### 3. Self-Compassion and Mistakes:

Emily practiced self-compassion when she made artistic mistakes. Instead of berating herself, she treated herself with kindness and understanding, recognizing that making mistakes was part of her creative journey.

### Building Resilience Through Adversity

As Emily continued to explore her passion for painting, life presented her with unforeseen challenges. A sudden health issue left her unable to paint for months. It was a period of adversity that tested her newfound resilience.

### 1. Adversity as an Opportunity:

Emily viewed her health setback as an opportunity for personal growth. She began reading about art, studying art history, and exploring different artistic styles from her bed.

### 2. Developing Resilience:

Through her reading and research, Emily developed resilience. She maintained a growth mindset, determined to return to painting once her health improved.

### 3. Learning from Setbacks:

Emily's resilience allowed her to learn from setbacks. When she finally regained her health, she returned to her art with newfound determination and a deeper appreciation for her craft.

### The Transformation

Emily's journey of embracing failure and building resilience transformed her life. She no longer feared making mistakes or falling short of external expectations. She embraced vulnerability in her art and personal life, allowing her true self to shine through.

Her paintings began to reflect her newfound authenticity. She didn't just create art; she poured her emotions, experiences, and vulnerability onto the canvas. Her work resonated with others, who saw the beauty in her imperfections and the depth of her self-expression.

But the most significant transformation was in Emily herself. She had shifted from a life driven by fear of failure to one fueled by the courage to embrace it. She understood resilience was not about avoiding adversity but navigating it with grace and resilience.

Emily's story is a powerful reminder of the transformative power of embracing failure and building resilience. It's a testament to the fact that setbacks are not the end of the road, but growth opportunities and that self-trust is nurtured through the willingness to learn from life's challenges and rise stronger each time.

# CHAPTER 7

## NURTURING INTUITION

"I'll not listen to reason... reason always means
what someone else has got to say."

—— **Elizabeth Gaskell**

—·—

## NURTURING INTUITION

- What Is Intuition?

- Honing Your Intuitive Abilities

- Listening to Your Gut Feeling

**What Is Intuition?**

Intuition is often described as a deep, instinctive feeling or understanding about something without the need for conscious reasoning. That inner voice guides us, the gut feeling that helps us make decisions, and the subtle nudges that provide insights beyond what we can rationally explain.

**1. Intuition as Inner Wisdom:**

Intuition is often referred to as our inner wisdom. It's the part of us that knows what's right or wrong, even when we can't logically explain it.

## 2. The Role of Intuition in Decision-Making:

Intuition plays a significant role in decision-making. It can help us choose a path, make choices, or avoid situations that don't align with our authentic selves.

## 3. Intuition and Creativity:

Intuition is closely tied to creativity. Many artists, writers, and innovators credit their intuitive insights for breakthroughs in their work.

## Honing Your Intuitive Abilities

Intuition is not a mysterious gift possessed by a select few; it's a skill that can be cultivated and developed over time. Here are steps to hone your intuitive abilities.

## 1. Quiet Your Mind:

Intuition often emerges when the mind is calm and still. Practice meditation, mindfulness, or simply spend time in nature to quiet the mental chatter.

## 2. Trust Your Feelings:

Start by paying attention to your emotions and feelings. Your body often communicates intuitive insights through physical sensations, such as gut feelings or unease.

### 3. Journaling:

Keep a journal to record your intuitive experiences. Over time, you may notice patterns or recurring themes that provide guidance.

### 4. Develop Self-Awareness:

Intuition is closely connected to self-awareness. The better you understand yourself, your values, and your desires, the more you can trust your intuitive guidance.

### 5. Embrace Creativity:

Engage in creative activities such as art, writing, or music. Creativity can enhance your intuitive abilities and provide a channel for intuitive insights to surface.

### Listening to Your Gut Feeling

Listening to your gut feeling is an essential aspect of nurturing intuition. It involves acknowledging and heeding the inner guidance that arises from your intuitive senses.

### 1. Recognize the Physical Signals:

Pay attention to physical sensations in your body. A tight feeling in the chest or a sense of excitement can be indicators of intuitive guidance.

## 2. Trust Your Initial Response:

Your first impression or reaction to a situation is often intuitive. Trust it before overanalyzing or seeking external opinions.

## 3. Test Your Intuition:

Start with small decisions where the consequences are not significant. Trust your intuition and see how it plays out. Over time, you'll build confidence in your intuitive abilities.

## 4. Be Patient:

Intuition only sometimes provides immediate answers. Sometimes, it requires patience and time to reveal its wisdom.

## The Intuitive Path to Self-Trust

Nurturing intuition is a profound journey toward self-trust. You trust yourself and your inner wisdom when you listen to your intuition and follow its guidance.

Intuition is not infallible, and it can coexist with rational decision-making. The key is to balance intuition and logic, allowing both to inform your choices.

In the chapters, we will explore practical exercises and strategies to develop your intuitive abilities further. Remember that intuition is a powerful tool for building self-trust and living a life that aligns with your authentic self. By nurturing your intuition, you unlock a deeper understanding of yourself and the world around you, guiding you toward greater fulfillment and authenticity.

### *Whispers of the Heart: A Journey of Nurturing Intuition*

Mary had always been drawn to the mysterious realm of intuition. She had a deep sense that there was more to life than what met the eye, and she was determined to uncover the hidden wisdom within her.

## What Is Intuition?

Mary's journey to nurture her intuition began with a quest for understanding. She wanted to grasp the essence of intuition, which often seemed elusive, like trying to catch a whisper in the wind.

## 1. Intuition as Subtle Wisdom:

Mary discovered intuition wasn't about loud proclamations but rather subtle whispers of wisdom. The quiet voice guided her when she allowed herself to listen.

## 2. Intuition in Decision-Making:

Mary realized that intuition played a vital role in her decision-making. That inner compass helped her choose her path, even when logic provided no clear answers.

### 3. Nurturing the Intuitive Spark:

As she explored intuition further, Mary found it was like a spark within her that could be ignited and nurtured with attention and practice.

### Honing Your Intuitive Abilities

Mary embarked on a journey of self-discovery, determined to hone her intuitive abilities. She understood that intuition, like any skill, could be developed over time.

### 1. Quieting the Mind:

Mary practiced meditation and mindfulness to quiet her busy mind. She discovered that in moments of stillness, her intuition was more accessible.

### 2. Embracing Emotions:

She learned to pay attention to her emotions and feelings, understanding that they were often the first signals of intuitive guidance. When something didn't feel right, she trusted her intuition to guide her away from it.

## 3. Keeping a Journal:

To track her progress, Mary kept a journal of her intuitive experiences. She noted moments when her inner voice had proven right and times when she'd ignored it to her detriment.

## 4. Deepening Self-Awareness:

Mary embarked on a journey of self-discovery, delving into her values, beliefs, and desires. She understood that the better she knew herself, the more in tune she would be with her intuition.

## Listening to Your Gut Feeling

One day, as Mary stood at a crossroads in her life, she received a job offer that seemed perfect on paper. Yet, her intuition sent her subtle warnings, a gut feeling that something wasn't right.

## 1. Recognizing the Physical Signals:

Mary paid close attention to the physical sensations in her body. Her gut tightened, and a sense of unease washed over her whenever she considered accepting the offer.

## 2. Trusting Her Initial Response:

Mary trusted her initial response, even though it went against conventional wisdom. She declined the job offer despite the pressure to accept it.

## 3. Embracing Patience:

Mary had to be patient. She accepted a seemingly perfect opportunity after knowing what lay ahead. But she trusted her intuition to guide her.

## The Transformation

Over time, Mary's intuitive abilities blossomed. She learned to listen to her inner voice, trust her gut feelings, and honor the subtle whispers of wisdom within her.

Her decision to decline the job offer proved to be a turning point. Shortly afterward, she stumbled upon a career opportunity that resonated deeply with her values and passions. It wasn't what society deemed the "perfect" job, but it was perfect for her.

Mary's story is a testament to the power of nurturing intuition. It's a reminder that intuition is not a mystical gift reserved for a select few but a skill that can be developed by anyone willing to listen to their inner wisdom. By nurturing her intuition, Mary found her authentic path and discovered a more profound sense of self-trust and authenticity that illuminated her journey through life.

# CHAPTER 8

## DEVELOPING SELF-CONFIDENCE

"Every path but your own is the path of fate.
Keep on your own track, then."

—— **Henry David Thoreau**

— • —

## DEVELOPING SELF-CONFIDENCE

- The Connection Between Self-Trust and Self-Confidence

- Building Confidence Through Competence

- Challenging Impostor Syndrome

### The Connection Between Self-Trust and Self-Confidence

Self-confidence is intrinsically linked to self-trust. When you trust yourself, you believe in your ability to make choices, take action, and handle whatever challenges come your way. This belief forms the foundation of self-confidence, and the two concepts reinforce and strengthen each other.

### 1. Trust as the Root of Confidence:

Self-trust serves as the root from which self-confidence can grow. When you trust your judgment and decisions, you naturally become more confident in your abilities.

## 2. Self-Confidence as a Feedback Loop:

Self-confidence, once cultivated, enhances self-trust. As you take confident actions and see positive outcomes, your self-trust deepens, allowing you to take even more confident steps.

## 3. The Role of Self-Doubt:

Self-doubt can erode both self-trust and self-confidence. You create a solid foundation to nurture self-confidence by addressing self-doubt and building self-trust.

## Building Confidence Through Competence

Competence is a critical component of self-confidence. Knowing you have the skills, knowledge, and abilities to succeed in a particular area bolsters your confidence.

## 1. Identify Your Strengths:

Begin by recognizing your strengths and talents. What are you naturally good at? What skills have you developed over time? Building on your strengths can boost your confidence.

## 2. Set Achievable Goals:

Break your larger goals into smaller, achievable steps. Each small success builds your confidence and demonstrates your competence.

## 3. Seek Education and Training:

Invest in learning and skill development. Expanding your knowledge through formal education, workshops, or self-study enhances your competence.

## 4. Embrace Challenges:

Please don't shy away from challenges; view them as opportunities to grow and demonstrate your competence. Overcoming obstacles can significantly boost self-confidence.

## Challenging Impostor Syndrome

Impostor syndrome is a common phenomenon in which individuals doubt their abilities and feel like a fraud despite evidence of competence. Overcoming impostor syndrome is essential for developing self-confidence.

## 1. Recognize Impostor Thoughts:

Start by recognizing when impostor thoughts arise. Become aware of the moments when you doubt your abilities or feel like a fraud.

## 2. Reframe Negative Self-Talk:

Challenge negative self-talk and replace it with more positive, realistic affirmations. Instead of thinking, "I don't deserve this," remind yourself of your qualifications and accomplishments.

## 3. Seek Support and Validation:

Share your feelings of impostor syndrome with trusted friends, mentors, or therapists. They can provide perspective and validation of your abilities.

## 4. Keep a Success Journal:

Document your achievements and successes in a journal. Reviewing your accomplishments can help counter feelings of inadequacy.

## The Path to Unshakeable Self-Confidence

Developing self-confidence is a transformative journey that complements and reinforces self-trust. It involves recognizing your worth, cultivating competence, and addressing self-doubt.

Self-confidence isn't about being free from doubt or never facing setbacks. Instead, it's about believing in yourself to navigate challenges and persevere in adversity. It's the unwavering faith in your ability to learn, adapt, and grow.

In the chapters ahead, we will explore practical exercises and strategies to help you boost your self-confidence, ultimately leading to a deeper sense of self-trust and authenticity. Remember that self-confidence, like self-trust, is a skill that can be developed and nurtured over time, leading to a more authentic and fulfilling life.

## *The Journey to Unshakable Confidence: A Story of Self-Trust and Triumph*

Jamie always grappled with self-doubt and lacked self-confidence. She yearned to bridge the gap between her potential and her self-perception, embarking on a transformative journey of self-trust and self-confidence.

## The Connection Between Self-Trust and Self-Confidence

Jamie's journey began with the realization that self-trust was intricately tied to self-confidence. She recognized that her lack of confidence stemmed from an underlying belief that she couldn't rely on herself.

## 1. Trust as a Building Block:

Jamie understood that self-trust served as a foundational building block for self-confidence. She needed to trust her judgment, decisions, and capabilities to be confident.

## 2. The Reciprocal Nature:

As Jamie built her self-confidence, she discovered it strengthened her self-trust. Each small victory bolstered her belief in her abilities and choices.

## 3. The Struggle with Self-Doubt:

Self-doubt had been a persistent companion in Jamie's life, undermining both her self-trust and self-confidence. She knew that addressing self-doubt was key to her transformation.

## Building Confidence Through Competence

To boost her self-confidence, Jamie embarked on a journey to enhance her competence. She realized that having the skills, knowledge, and experience in her chosen areas of interest would bolster her confidence.

## 1. Identifying Strengths:

Jamie took time to identify her strengths and talents. She acknowledged her ability to communicate effectively and her aptitude for problem-solving.

## 2. Setting Achievable Goals:

She set clear, achievable goals, breaking them into smaller, manageable steps. Each accomplishment became a building block for her self-confidence.

## 3. Continuous Learning:

Jamie pursued education and training in areas she was passionate about. Gaining knowledge and expertise boosted her competence.

## 4. Embracing Challenges:

Instead of shying away from challenges, Jamie embraced them. She saw each obstacle as an opportunity to prove her competence and build self-confidence.

## Challenging Impostor Syndrome

Jamie's path to self-confidence wasn't without its challenges, and one of the most significant hurdles she faced was impostor syndrome. She often felt like a fraud despite her accomplishments.

## 1. Recognizing Impostor Thoughts:

Jamie began recognizing impostor thoughts as they emerged. She would pause, acknowledge them, and then challenge their validity.

## 2. Reframing Negative Self-Talk:

She worked on reframing her negative self-talk. Instead of thinking she didn't deserve her achievements, she celebrated her hard work and dedication.

## 3. Seeking Support:

Jamie confided in a close friend about her impostor syndrome. Sharing her feelings with someone she trusted provided validation and perspective.

## 4. Success Journal:

She started keeping a journal of her successes and achievements. Revisiting her accomplishments served as a reminder of her competence and silenced her inner impostor.

## The Transformation

Over time, Jamie's journey bore fruit. Her self-trust deepened, and her self-confidence blossomed. She began to see herself as a capable, competent individual deserving of success.

As her self-confidence grew, Jamie pursued opportunities she once deemed out of reach. She excelled in her career, took on leadership roles, and became a mentor to others grappling with self-doubt. Her transformation served as an inspiration to many.

Jamie's story is a testament to the transformative power of developing self-confidence. It underscores the close connection between self-trust and self-confidence, emphasizing that both can be nurtured and strengthened. By addressing self-doubt, cultivating competence, and challenging impostor syndrome, Jamie became more confident and lived a more authentic and fulfilling life.

# CHAPTER 9

## CULTIVATING HEALTHY BOUNDARIES

"Self trust is the essence of heroism."

—— **Ralph Waldo Emerson**

—·—

— • —

## CULTIVATING HEALTHY BOUNDARIES

- The Role of Boundaries in Self-Trust

- Setting and Communicating Boundaries

- Respecting the Boundaries of Others

**The Role of Boundaries in Self-Trust**

Boundaries are the invisible lines that define acceptable behavior and interaction limits in our lives. Cultivating healthy boundaries is paramount to building self-trust. Boundaries serve as the framework for protecting our emotional, mental, and physical well-being.

**1. Self-Respect and Boundaries:**

Healthy boundaries reflect self-respect. When we set boundaries, we signal to ourselves and others that our needs, values, and emotions matter.

## 2. Trusting Your Instincts:

Boundaries enable us to trust our instincts and intuition. They provide a clear framework for evaluating situations and making choices aligned with our authentic selves.

## 3. Building Self-Esteem:

The ability to set and maintain boundaries is linked to self-esteem. As we assert our boundaries, we reinforce our self-worth and develop self-trust.

## Setting and Communicating Boundaries

Creating and communicating boundaries is a proactive and empowering process. It involves defining what is acceptable to you and effectively expressing these limits to others.

## 1. Self-Reflection:

Begin by reflecting on your needs, values, and what makes you feel comfortable or uncomfortable in various situations. This self-awareness forms the basis of your boundaries.

## 2. Define Your Boundaries:

Clearly articulate your boundaries in specific terms. For example, you might set personal space, time, emotional intimacy, or communication boundaries.

### 3. Communicate Effectively:

Communicate your boundaries assertively and with kindness. Use "I" statements to express your needs and explain why the boundary is important to you.

### 4. Enforce Your Boundaries:

Consistently uphold your boundaries by taking action when they are crossed. This may involve calmly but firmly reasserting your boundaries or creating distance from those who repeatedly disrespect them.

### Respecting the Boundaries of Others

As you cultivate healthy boundaries, it's equally important to respect the boundaries of others. Mutual respect fosters trust and healthy relationships.

### 1. Active Listening:

Please pay attention when others express their boundaries. Listen actively and empathetically to understand their needs and concerns.

### 2. Ask for Clarification:

If you're unsure about someone's boundaries, don't hesitate to ask for clarification. This demonstrates your respect for their autonomy.

## 3. Avoid Assumptions:

Avoid making assumptions about what others are comfortable with. Instead, seek their input and consent in various situations.

## 4. Apologize and Adjust:

If you inadvertently cross someone's boundaries, apologize sincerely and adjust your behavior accordingly. Recognizing that everyone makes mistakes and taking responsibility builds trust.

## The Liberating Power of Healthy Boundaries

Cultivating and maintaining healthy boundaries is an act of self-care and self-trust. It liberates us from harmful dynamics, empowers us to make choices aligned with our values, and strengthens our relationships.

Healthy boundaries enable us to:

## 1. Protect Your Well-Being:

Boundaries safeguard your emotional and mental well-being, ensuring that you engage in relationships and situations that are nurturing rather than draining.

## 2. Foster Authenticity:

Setting boundaries allows you to be authentic and true to yourself. You no longer compromise your values or conform to others' expectations.

## 3. Enhance Self-Trust:

As you consistently respect and enforce your boundaries, your self-trust deepens. You become confident in making choices that serve your best interests.

## 4. Nurture Healthy Relationships:

Healthy boundaries are the cornerstone of healthy relationships. They encourage open communication, mutual respect, and the growth of trust within connections.

## The Journey to Boundaries and Self-Trust

Cultivating healthy boundaries is a journey that intertwines with the development of self-trust. It is a process of self-discovery, self-advocacy, and self-care. As you navigate this journey, remember that boundaries are not walls but bridges—bridges that connect you to your authentic self and to others in a way that fosters trust, respect, and well-being.

### *Boundaries of the Heart: A Journey to Self-Trust*

Emma embarked on a profound journey of self-discovery and self-trust in a picturesque town nestled by the sea. Her story beautifully illustrates the transformative power of cultivating healthy boundaries.

## The Role of Boundaries in Self-Trust

Emma's journey began when she felt overwhelmed and drained in her relationships. She realized she had neglected to set clear boundaries, often putting others' needs before hers.

### 1. Recognizing the Need for Boundaries:

Emma understood that boundaries were essential for self-trust. She recognized that by failing to set boundaries, she was compromising her own well-being.

### 2. Trusting Her Feelings:

Emma began to trust her feelings and instincts. She acknowledged that feeling uncomfortable in certain situations was a sign that her boundaries had been crossed.

### 3. Building Self-Respect:

As Emma set and enforced her boundaries, her self-respect grew. She realized that respecting her own needs and values was an essential element of self-trust.

## Setting and Communicating Boundaries

Emma embarked on the journey of setting and communicating her boundaries. She knew that this was essential not only for her own well-being but also for nurturing healthy relationships.

### 1. Self-Reflection:

Emma engaged in self-reflection to understand her needs, values, and triggers. This self-awareness was the foundation of her boundaries.

### 2. Defining Her Boundaries:

Emma clearly defined her boundaries for herself and those close to her. She realized that boundaries were not walls but necessary guidelines.

### 3. Assertive Communication:

Emma learned to communicate her boundaries assertively and kindly. She used "I" statements to express her needs and explained why these boundaries were important to her.

### 4. Consistency and Self-Care:

Emma consistently enforced her boundaries. She realized that self-care was vital to maintaining healthy boundaries and self-trust.

## Respecting the Boundaries of Others

As Emma learned to set and communicate her boundaries, she also embraced the importance of respecting the boundaries of others.

## 1. Active Listening:

Emma became an active listener, paying attention when others shared their boundaries. She was attentive and empathetic to their needs.

## 2. Seeking Clarity:

When in doubt about someone else's boundaries, Emma asked for clarification. This demonstrated her respect for their autonomy.

## 3. Avoiding Assumptions:

Emma stopped making assumptions about what others were comfortable with. Instead, she sought their input and consent in various situations.

## 4. Apologizing and Adjusting:

Emma sincerely apologized and adjusted her behavior if she unintentionally crossed someone's boundaries. She understood that respecting boundaries was a two-way street.

## The Transformation

As Emma consistently set and respected boundaries, her life began to change. She noticed a profound shift in her relationships. Those who genuinely cared for her respected her boundaries, and her connections deepened.

Emma's self-trust grew steadily. She learned that her needs and values were essential and deserving of respect. This newfound self-trust allowed her to navigate life's challenges confidently and authentically.

Her journey inspired those around her to reflect on their own boundaries and the role they played in nurturing self-trust and healthy connections.

## Boundaries of the Heart

Emma's story is a testament to the transformative power of cultivating healthy boundaries. It illustrates the profound connection between boundaries and self-trust, emphasizing that setting, communicating, and respecting boundaries are essential steps toward living a life that aligns with one's authentic self. Emma's journey serves as a beacon of hope for those seeking to nurture self-trust through the liberating embrace of boundaries.

# CHAPTER 10

## SURROUNDING YOURSELF WITH SUPPORT

"Accept the pain for what it is and focus
more completely on what you want."

—— **Adeleke Aishat**

—·—

— • —

# Surrounding Yourself with Support

- Building a Supportive Network

- The Importance of Vulnerability

- Seeking Professional Help When Needed

## Building a Supportive Network

One of the cornerstones of self-trust and personal growth is the presence of a supportive network. Surrounding yourself with people who genuinely care for your well-being and encourage your authentic self is invaluable.

## 1. Identifying Supportive Relationships:

The first step is recognizing and nurturing existing relationships that are supportive and nourishing. These may include friends, family members, or mentors who have your best interests at heart.

## 2. Cultivating New Connections:

Actively seek out individuals who share your values and passions. Join clubs, groups, or communities that align with your interests, where you can form new, supportive connections.

## 3. Mutual Respect and Empathy:

A supportive network is built on mutual respect and empathy. It's a space where you can be vulnerable and authentic without fear of judgment.

## 4. Setting Boundaries:

While seeking support, it's essential to maintain healthy boundaries. A supportive network respects your boundaries and encourages you to communicate your needs.

## The Importance of Vulnerability

Vulnerability is the key to deepening relationships and fostering self-trust. It involves sharing your authentic self, fears, dreams, and imperfections with others.

## 1. Overcoming Fear:

Vulnerability requires facing the fear of rejection and judgment. It's about acknowledging that being authentic means being imperfect.

## 2. Strengthening Connections:

Sharing your vulnerabilities with others can strengthen your relationships. It builds trust, showing that you trust the other person enough to let them see your true self.

## 3. Self-Validation:

Vulnerability is also about validating your own emotions and experiences. By being vulnerable with yourself, you deepen your self-trust and self-acceptance.

## 4. Encouraging Authenticity:

When you are vulnerable, you encourage others to be authentic in return. This fosters an environment of openness and support.

## Seeking Professional Help When Needed

While friends and family provide valuable support, there are times when seeking professional help is necessary for personal growth and healing.

## 1. Recognizing the Need:

It's essential to recognize when you need professional help, whether it's for mental health issues, trauma, addiction, or any other challenging situation.

## 2. Breaking Stigmas:

Seeking professional help is a courageous step that breaks stigmas surrounding mental health. It's a sign of self-care and self-respect.

## 3. Expert Guidance:

Professionals such as therapists, counselors, and coaches offer expert guidance and tools to help you navigate challenges and build self-trust.

## 4. Complementing Support Network:

Professional help can complement your support network, providing a different perspective and specialized strategies for your unique needs.

## The Power of a Supportive Network

A supportive network is vital in your journey toward self-trust and authenticity. It provides encouragement, validation, and a safe space for you to explore your true self.

## 1. Emotional Resilience:

A supportive network helps you develop emotional resilience. When you face challenges, your network provides a safety net, reminding you that you are not alone.

## 2. Affirmation of Self-Worth:

Your support network affirms your self-worth. They remind you of your value and strengths when self-doubt creeps in.

### 3. Encouragement to Grow:

Surrounding yourself with support encourages you to take risks, embrace change, and grow. It's a constant reminder that you are capable of transformation.

### 4. Celebration of Authenticity:

Your support network celebrates your authentic self. They appreciate you for who you are, not who you think you should be.

### Nurturing Self-Trust through Support

In your quest to build self-trust and authenticity, remember you don't have to go it alone. A strong support network, a willingness to be vulnerable, and recognizing when professional help is needed are essential elements of this transformative journey.

Your support network becomes the mirror through which you see your authentic self-reflection and the cushion that softens life's challenges. It's a testament to the power of human connection and a reminder that self-trust is nurtured through the love, understanding, and encouragement of those around you.

### *Bridges of Support: A Journey to Self-Trust*

Lisa found herself at a crossroads in her life. Her journey to self-trust and authenticity was inextricably linked to the support network she cultivated along the way.

## Building a Supportive Network

Lisa had always been a fiercely independent person, believing that she could tackle any challenge on her own. However, as she delved deeper into her journey of self-discovery, she realized the significance of a supportive network.

### 1. Rediscovering Old Bonds:

Lisa began by reconnecting with old friends and family members. These people had known her longest and could provide a sense of familiarity and unconditional support.

### 2. The Power of New Friendships:

Lisa joined clubs and organizations related to her interests. In doing so, she formed new, meaningful friendships with like-minded individuals who shared her passions.

### 3. Mutual Respect and Empathy:

Her network was characterized by mutual respect and empathy. It was a safe space to express her thoughts, fears, and desires without fear of judgment.

## 4. Setting Boundaries:

Lisa learned to set and communicate her boundaries as she built her support network. She realized that maintaining healthy limits was crucial for her well-being and her relationships' health.

## The Importance of Vulnerability

Lisa's journey also entailed embracing vulnerability—a step she had long avoided. She began to share her true self, including her fears, insecurities, and dreams, with those she trusted.

## 1. Confronting Fear:

Vulnerability required Lisa to confront her fear of rejection and judgment. She realized that being authentic meant being open to vulnerability.

## 2. Strengthening Connections:

Sharing her vulnerabilities deepened her connections with others. It created a sense of trust and allowed people to see her for who she truly was.

## 3. Self-Validation:

Lisa's vulnerability was also a form of self-validation. She built a stronger sense of self-trust and self-acceptance by accepting and embracing her own emotions and experiences.

## 4. Encouraging Authenticity:

Lisa's willingness to be vulnerable also encouraged those around her to be authentic. It fostered an environment of openness and mutual support.

## Seeking Professional Help When Needed

Throughout her journey, Lisa encountered challenges beyond the realm of what her support network could address. In these instances, she recognized the importance of seeking professional help.

## 1. Recognizing the Need:

Lisa learned to recognize when she needed professional help, such as therapy or counseling, to navigate her mental and emotional well-being issues.

## 2. Breaking Stigmas:

Seeking professional help was a significant step in breaking stigmas surrounding mental health. Lisa viewed it as an act of self-care and self-respect.

## 3. Expert Guidance:

Professionals provided Lisa with expert guidance and tools to address specific challenges. Their support complemented the care and understanding she received from her personal network.

## 4. Complementing Support Network:

Lisa understood that professional help complemented her support network. It offered a different perspective and specialized strategies tailored to her unique needs.

## The Power of a Supportive Network

Lisa's journey was marked by profound transformation. Her support network was pivotal in her quest for self-trust and authenticity.

## 1. Emotional Resilience:

Lisa's support network helped her develop emotional resilience. When facing challenges, her network served as a safety net, reminding her she was not alone.

## 2. Affirmation of Self-Worth:

Her friends and loved ones affirmed her self-worth. They reminded her of her value and strengths during moments of self-doubt.

## 3. Encouragement to Grow:

Lisa's support network encouraged her to take risks, embrace change, and grow as a person. It served as a constant reminder that she was capable of transformation.

## 4. Celebration of Authenticity:

Her network celebrated her authentic self. They appreciated her for who she was, not who she thought she should be.

## Nurturing Self-Trust through Support

In her journey to self-trust and authenticity, Lisa learned she didn't have to go it alone. A strong support network, a willingness to be vulnerable, and recognizing when professional help was needed were essential elements of her transformation.

Lisa's support network became the mirror through which she saw her authentic self reflected and the cushion that softened life's challenges. It was a testament to the power of human connection and a reminder that self-trust is nurtured through the love, understanding, and encouragement of those around you.

— · —

# Chapter 11

## Embracing Change and Growth

"Blessed are the flexible, for change is inevitable.
To fulfill our true destiny as spiritual beings we
must trust in our divine power to adapt."

—— **Anthon St. Maarten**

—·—

# EMBRACING CHANGE AND GROWTH

- The Nature of Change

- Embracing Personal Growth

- Letting Go of the Past

## The Nature of Change

Change is a fundamental and constant aspect of life. The force propels us forward, whether we're ready or not. Embracing change is essential for building self-trust and leading an authentic life.

## 1. Impermanence of Life:

Change reminds us of the impermanence of life. Nothing stays the same forever, and accepting this truth is the first step in embracing change.

## 2. Catalyst for Transformation:

Change catalyzes personal growth and self-discovery. It pushes us out of our comfort zones and encourages us to evolve.

## 3. Overcoming Fear:

Embracing change requires confronting the fear of the unknown. It teaches us to manage uncertainty and build resilience in facing challenges.

## 4. Opportunity for Reinvention:

Change provides an opportunity for reinvention. It allows us to shed old identities and step into new, more authentic versions of ourselves.

## Embracing Personal Growth

Personal growth is the intentional and continuous process of becoming the best version of yourself. It's about learning, evolving, and expanding your potential.

## 1. Self-Awareness:

Personal growth starts with self-awareness. It involves recognizing your strengths, weaknesses, values, and desires.

## 2. Goal Setting:

Setting clear, achievable goals is a crucial part of personal growth. These goals give you direction and purpose on your journey.

## 3. Lifelong Learning:

Embrace a mindset of lifelong learning. Seek new knowledge, skills, and experiences to fuel your personal growth.

## 4. Resilience and Adaptability:

Personal growth builds resilience and adaptability. It helps you navigate life's challenges with grace and determination.

## Letting Go of the Past

One of the most challenging aspects of change and growth is letting go of the past. It requires releasing attachments to what no longer serves you and making space for new possibilities.

## 1. Forgiveness and Healing:

Letting go often involves forgiving yourself and others for past mistakes or hurts. This process is essential for emotional healing and personal growth.

## 2. Detoxifying Your Life:

Identify and eliminate toxic relationships, habits, or beliefs that are holding you back. Creating space for positive influences is crucial for growth.

## 3. Present-Moment Focus:

Practice mindfulness and being present. Letting go of the past means embracing the beauty and potential of the present moment.

## 4. Embracing Change as an Opportunity:

Shift your perspective on change. Instead of fearing it, see it as an opportunity for growth and renewal.

## The Dance of Change and Growth

Change and personal growth are intrinsically linked. They form a dynamic dance in which each step forward is propelled by the willingness to embrace change.

## 1. Embracing Discomfort:

Personal growth often involves stepping out of your comfort zone. It requires facing discomfort and uncertainty head-on.

## 2. Learning from Adversity:

Some of the most profound personal growth occurs during times of adversity. These challenges are opportunities to test your resilience and adaptability.

## 3. Celebrating Progress:

Acknowledge and celebrate your growth. Each small step forward is a testament to your strength and determination.

## 4. Embracing Authenticity:

As you grow, you become more authentic. Personal growth allows you to shed societal expectations and embrace your true self.

## The Continuous Journey

Embracing change and personal growth is not a one-time event but a continuous journey. It's a commitment to evolving, learning, and becoming more authentic with each passing day.

## 1. The Beauty of Uncertainty:

Learn to appreciate the beauty of uncertainty. In these moments of not knowing what lies ahead, you often discover your truest self.

## 2. Compassionate Self-Reflection:

Regularly reflect on your journey. Be kind to yourself, acknowledging that growth sometimes involves setbacks and detours.

## 3. Supporting Others:

Extend your support to others on their journey of change and personal growth. Building a community of growth-minded individuals fosters a sense of belonging and shared purpose.

## 4. The Endless Potential:

Understand that your potential for change and growth is endless. Each step you take opens doors to new possibilities and a deeper sense of self-trust and authenticity.

## Embrace the Dance

Embracing change and personal growth is the dance of a lifetime. It's a dance that leads you toward self-trust, authenticity, and a more prosperous, more meaningful existence. So, step onto the dance floor of life, embrace the rhythm of change, and let your personal growth be the melody that guides you toward a more authentic and fulfilling future.

### *Rebirth: A Journey of Change and Personal Growth*

Shannon had spent most of her life resisting change. She was comfortable in her routine, surrounded by the familiar, but deep inside, she knew something was missing. Her journey of embracing change and personal growth was about to begin.

## The Nature of Change

Shannon's realization that change was inevitable dawned on her when she faced a sudden job loss. She had worked for the same company for over a decade, and starting anew was daunting. Change had knocked on her door, and she had no choice but to answer.

### 1. The Unpredictable Nature:

Change often comes uninvited and unpredictable, but the unpredictability makes life exciting and full of possibilities.

### 2. Catalyst for Transformation:

Shannon realized that change could be a catalyst for personal growth. It challenged her to adapt, learn new skills, and reevaluate her goals.

### 3. Overcoming Fear:

Embracing change meant confronting her fear of the unknown. She learned that stepping out of her comfort zone could conquer those fears and build self-trust.

### 4. Opportunity for Reinvention:

The change offered Shannon the chance to reinvent herself. She could let go of the past and redefine her identity on her own terms.

## Embracing Personal Growth

Shannon's journey into personal growth began when she decided to return to school to pursue a different career. It was a daunting prospect for someone who had been out of the academic world for years, but Shannon was determined.

### 1. Self-Awareness:

Personal growth started with self-awareness. Shannon examined her interests, strengths, and weaknesses to choose a path that resonated with her authentic self.

### 2. Goal Setting:

She set clear goals for herself. Her guiding objectives were completing her education, acquiring new skills, and building a new career.

### 3. Lifelong Learning:

Shannon embraced a mindset of lifelong learning. She was excited about acquiring new knowledge and skill sets to find fulfillment in the process.

## 4. Resilience and Adaptability:

Her personal growth journey cultivated resilience and adaptability. Shannon learned to embrace change as a natural part of life, making her more agile in facing challenges.

## Letting Go of the Past

Shannon's journey also required letting go of the past, including the security of her old job and her attachment to a career she had known for years. This process was both liberating and challenging.

## 1. Forgiveness and Healing:

She had to forgive herself for any regrets and let go of any bitterness. This act of forgiveness brought healing and peace.

## 2. Detoxifying Your Life:

Shannon also had to detoxify her life of unhealthy habits and relationships. She distanced herself from those who held her back and created space for positive influences.

## 3. Present-Moment Focus:

Embracing change meant being present. Shannon realized that dwelling on the past or worrying about the future hindered her personal growth.

## 4. Embracing Change as an Opportunity:

Finally, she began to see change as an opportunity for growth rather than a loss. It was a chance to leave behind what didn't serve her and move toward her authentic self.

## The Continuous Journey

Shannon's journey of embracing change and personal growth wasn't a one-time event but a continuous process. It was a commitment to evolving, learning, and becoming a more authentic version of herself each day.

## 1. The Beauty of Uncertainty:

She learned to appreciate the beauty of uncertainty. She discovered her true self in these moments of not knowing what lay ahead.

## 2. Compassionate Self-Reflection:

Regular self-reflection allowed Shannon to acknowledge and celebrate her growth, even during setbacks and detours.

## 3. Supporting Others:

Shannon supported others on their journey of change and personal growth. She knew that building a community of growth-minded individuals fostered a sense of belonging and shared purpose.

## 4. The Endless Potential:

She understood that her potential for change and growth was endless. With each step, she opened doors to new possibilities and a deeper sense of self-trust and authenticity.

## The Blossoming

Shannon's journey was not without its challenges, but she blossomed into a woman who trusted herself and lived authentically through embracing change and personal growth. Her transformation was a testament to the power of change as a force for self-discovery and growth. Shannon learned that change wasn't something to be feared but an opportunity to become her best version.

# CHAPTER 12

## LIVING A LIFE OF AUTHENTICITY

"Listen to that inner voice of yours.
It's not you, but it's for you."

—— **Kiyo Giaozhi**

—— • ——

## Living a Life of Authenticity

- The Rewards of Self-Trust

- Expressing Your Authentic Self

- Inspiring Others Through Your Journey

### The Rewards of Self-Trust

Living a life of authenticity is a reward in itself and the culmination of your journey to self-trust. When you trust yourself completely and embrace your true self, you unlock a world of rewards that profoundly enrich your life.

### 1. Inner Peace:

Self-trust brings a profound sense of inner peace. When you know you can rely on yourself, you let go of anxiety and self-doubt.

### 2. Confidence:

Self-trust builds unshakeable confidence. You believe in your abilities and decisions, which radiates in your interactions with others.

## 3. Fulfillment:

Authentic living leads to a sense of fulfillment. You align your choices and actions with your values and passions, resulting in a more satisfying life.

## 4. Resilience:

Self-trust fosters resilience. You bounce back from setbacks and face challenges with optimism and strength.

## Expressing Your Authentic Self

Living authentically means expressing your true self in every aspect of your life, from your relationships to your career. It's a conscious choice to be genuine and unapologetically you.

## 1. Authentic Relationships:

Authentic living fosters authentic relationships. You attract like-minded individuals who appreciate and accept you for who you are.

## 2. Professional Fulfillment:

In your career, authenticity leads to professional fulfillment. You choose paths and roles that align with your passions and values.

### 3. Self-Expression:

Authenticity is about self-expression. You find creative and meaningful ways to express your true self through art, writing, or other forms of creativity.

### 4. No More Pretense:

You shed the need for pretense or conformity. You no longer feel the pressure to be someone you're not to fit in or meet societal expectations.

### Inspiring Others Through Your Journey

As you live authentically and trust yourself fully, you inspire others. Your journey of self-discovery and self-trust can motivate and guide those around you.

### 1. Leading by Example:

Your authenticity leads by example. Others witness the positive transformation in your life and are encouraged to embark on their own journey of self-discovery.

### 2. Fostering Empathy:

Your vulnerability and authenticity foster empathy in your relationships. Others feel safe to share their true selves, deepening your connections.

## 3. A Ripple Effect:

Your journey's impact extends beyond your immediate circle. It creates a ripple effect, inspiring individuals you may never meet directly.

## 4. Supporting Growth:

By embracing your authenticity, you become a pillar of support for others. You encourage them to face their fears, embrace change, and build self-trust.

## Navigating the Challenges

Living a life of authenticity means life will be challenging. Authenticity often brings its own set of challenges as you confront societal norms and expectations.

## 1. Dealing with Judgment:

You may face judgment or criticism from those who don't understand or appreciate your authentic choices. Remember that their opinions don't define your worth.

## 2. Embracing Vulnerability:

Authenticity requires vulnerability. You may sometimes feel exposed or uncertain, but these moments are growth opportunities.

## 3. Navigating Change:

Embracing authenticity often involves significant life changes. You'll need to navigate these transitions with courage and resilience.

## 4. Embracing Imperfection:

Authentic living means embracing imperfection. You'll make mistakes, but these are valuable learning experiences on your journey.

## The Ongoing Journey

Living authentically is not a destination but an ongoing journey. It's a commitment to self-discovery, self-trust, and the continuous expression of your true self.

## 1. Cultivating Self-Compassion:

Be kind and compassionate to yourself as you navigate this journey. Self-compassion allows you to embrace your imperfections with love.

## 2. Embracing Change:

Continue to embrace change as an opportunity for growth. Be open to new experiences and challenges that expand your authenticity.

## 3. Nurturing Relationships:

Foster authentic connections with others who share your values and beliefs. These relationships provide support and encouragement.

## 4. Reflecting and Evolving:

Regular self-reflection allows you to evolve as you gain deeper insights into your true self. Celebrate your growth and adapt as needed.

## A Life of Fulfillment

Living a life of authenticity is a path to profound fulfillment and self-realization. It's a journey that rewards you with inner peace, confidence, and resilience while inspiring and supporting those around you. As you continue on this journey, remember that your authentic self is a gift to the world, and you genuinely shine through embracing it.

### *True Colors: A Journey to Living Authentically*

Claire had hidden her true self behind a façade of conformity for much of her life. But as time passed, she embarked on a transformative journey towards living authentically.

## The Rewards of Self-Trust

Claire's journey to authenticity began when she decided to trust herself completely. For years, she had sought external validation and approval, but deep down, she knew that true happiness could only come from self-trust.

### 1. Inner Peace:

As Claire started trusting herself, she discovered a profound inner peace. The constant turmoil of self-doubt began to dissipate, leaving her feeling grounded and serene.

### 2. Confidence:

Self-trust gave birth to unshakeable confidence within Claire. She began believing in her abilities, choices, and judgments, which radiated in her interactions.

### 3. Fulfillment:

Authentic living led to a sense of fulfillment that Claire had never known before. She aligned her choices and actions with her deepest values and passions, resulting in a more satisfying life.

## 4. Resilience:

Claire's self-trust fostered resilience. She learned to view challenges not as insurmountable obstacles but as opportunities for growth. This newfound resilience allowed her to face adversity with strength and grace.

## Expressing Your Authentic Self

Claire's journey also involved expressing her authentic self in every facet of her life. It meant making conscious choices to be genuine, regardless of the situation.

## 1. Authentic Relationships:

Authentic living fosters authentic relationships. Claire attracted like-minded individuals who appreciated and accepted her for who she truly was.

## 2. Professional Fulfillment:

In her career, Claire found professional fulfillment. She decided to pursue a path that resonated with her passions and values, bringing her a deep sense of purpose.

## 3. Self-Expression:

Authenticity was about self-expression for Claire. She found creative and meaningful ways to express her true self, from writing poetry to volunteering for causes she sincerely cared about.

## 4. No More Pretense:

Claire had shed the need for pretense or conformity. She no longer felt the pressure to be someone she wasn't to fit in or meet societal expectations.

## Inspiring Others Through Your Journey

Claire's journey towards authenticity had a profound impact on those around her. As she lived authentically and trusted herself fully, she inspired others.

## 1. Leading by Example:

Claire led by example. Friends and family witnessed the positive transformation in her life and were encouraged to embark on their own journey of self-discovery.

## 2. Fostering Empathy:

Her vulnerability and authenticity fostered empathy in her relationships. Loved ones felt safe to share their true selves, deepening their connections with Claire.

## 3. A Ripple Effect:

Claire's journey extended beyond her immediate circle. Her story inspired individuals she had never met directly, as her authenticity resonated with people from all walks of life.

## 4. Supporting Growth:

By embracing her authenticity, Claire became a pillar of support for others. She encouraged them to face their fears, embrace change, and build self-trust, just as she had done.

## Navigating the Challenges

Living authentically came with challenges for Claire. She had to confront judgment, navigate uncertainty, and embrace vulnerability.

## 1. Dealing with Judgment:

Claire faced judgment and criticism from those who didn't understand or appreciate her authentic choices. However, she remained steadfast, knowing that others' opinions didn't define her worth.

## 2. Embracing Vulnerability:

Authenticity required Claire to embrace vulnerability. She had moments of feeling exposed and uncertain, but she saw these moments as opportunities for growth.

## 3. Navigating Change:

Authentic living often involves significant life changes. Claire had to navigate these transitions with courage and resilience, knowing they were essential for her growth.

## 4. Embracing Imperfection:

Claire learned that embracing her authentic self meant embracing imperfection. She made mistakes but saw these as valuable learning experiences on her journey.

## The Ongoing Journey

Claire's journey towards authenticity was not a destination but an ongoing process. She continued to self-reflect, adapt, and grow as she gained more profound insights into her true self.

## 1. Cultivating Self-Compassion:

Claire practiced self-compassion, being kind and loving to herself as she navigated this journey. Self-compassion allowed her to embrace her imperfections with grace.

## 2. Embracing Change:

She continued to embrace change as an opportunity for growth. Claire was open to new experiences and challenges, which expanded her authenticity.

## 3. Nurturing Relationships:

Claire fostered authentic connections with those who shared her values and beliefs. These relationships provided unwavering support and encouragement.

## 4. Reflecting and Evolving:

She engaged in regular self-reflection to acknowledge and celebrate her growth, even in moments of setbacks and detours. Claire understood that growth was a continuous, evolving process.

## A Life of Fulfillment

Claire's journey towards living authentically transformed her life in profound ways. Her inner peace, unwavering confidence, sense of fulfillment, and resilience were testaments to the power of self-trust and authenticity.

As she continued this journey, Claire understood that her authentic self was a gift to the world. By embracing her true self and trusting her instincts, she found fulfillment and became an inspiration to those around her, reminding them that they, too, could live a life true to themselves. Claire's story illuminated the path to authenticity, showing that it was both attainable and deeply rewarding.

## CONCLUSION

*Continuously Nurturing Self-Trust*

As you reach the end of this transformative journey towards self-trust, authenticity, and personal growth, it's essential to take a moment to celebrate your progress. Your dedication, courage, and commitment to becoming authentic have led you to this point, a remarkable achievement.

### Celebrating Your Progress

Take a deep breath and reflect on how far you've come. Recall the moments of self-discovery, the challenges you've faced head-on, and the moments of vulnerability that have allowed you to connect with your true self. Celebrate the inner peace, confidence, and fulfillment that now grace your life, thanks to your unwavering pursuit of self-trust and authenticity.

### Continuously Nurturing Self-Trust

Remember that the journey doesn't end here; it merely evolves. Self-trust and authenticity are not fixed destinations but ongoing processes. The commitment to self-reflection, self-compassion, and personal growth will continue to serve as your compass on this ever-unfolding path.

Continue to embrace change, express your true self, and inspire others through your journey. Be prepared to face challenges and setbacks, for they are part of the human experience. During these moments, your self-trust will shine most brightly, guiding you through the storms and uncertainties of life.

## Encouragement for the Journey Ahead

As you move forward, know you are not alone on this journey. You are part of a community dedicated to living authentically and supporting one another. Your authenticity is a beacon of hope and inspiration for those who have yet to embark on their own path.

Take each step with courage; knowing your authentic self is your greatest asset. Your journey can impact your life and the lives of those you touch. Embrace your true colors, express your unique voice, and continue to cultivate self-trust as you navigate the beautiful, winding road ahead.

May your life be a testament to the transformative power of authenticity and self-trust. May you find fulfillment, purpose, and boundless joy as you continue to live a life that is true to your heart and soul.

# APPENDIX A: PRACTICAL ACTIVITIES TO ENHANCE SELF-TRUST

Self-trust is about inner belief and cultivating practical habits and activities that reinforce your confidence in yourself. The following exercises and activities are designed to help you build and enhance your self-trust in everyday life:**Exercise 1: Keep a Self-Trust Journal**

**Daily Self-Trust Reflection:** This daily practice invites you to set aside a dedicated time each day for introspection. Reflect on the moments when you trusted yourself during the day. These moments could range from making big and small decisions to acting on your intuition. Consider the outcomes of these self-trusting actions and decisions. Did they align with your values? Were they beneficial? By celebrating even the smallest instances of self-trust, you acknowledge your growth and reinforce your belief in your abilities.

**Self-Trust Tracking:** This journal section records instances when self-doubt crept in and influenced your choices or actions. Over time, review these entries and analyze whether your doubts were justified or rooted in unfounded fears or insecurities. By objectively examining these moments, you gain insights into self-doubt triggers and can work towards addressing them effectively.

**Identify Patterns:** As you accumulate entries in your self-trust journal, take time to reflect on patterns. Are there specific areas of your life where you struggle to trust yourself more than others? It could be related to work, relationships, health, or personal goals. Recognizing these patterns allows you to target specific areas for improvement and tailor your self-trust-building strategies accordingly.**Exercise 2: Build Competence**

**Skill Development:** Building self-trust is not solely about inner belief but also about tangible competence. Choose a skill or area in your life where you'd like to improve or gain expertise. Dedicate time regularly to learning and enhancing this skill. Whether it's a professional skill, a hobby, or a personal quality like patience or communication, as your skills grow, so will your self-trust. Confidence often stems from competence.

**Set Achievable Goals:** Break down your larger life goals into smaller, manageable steps. These smaller goals should be specific, measurable, achievable, relevant, and time-bound (SMART). As you accomplish these smaller milestones, your confidence in your ability to achieve more significant goals will naturally grow. This step-by-step approach builds competence and strengthens your belief in your capacity to navigate complex endeavors.

**Seek Feedback:** Don't hesitate to seek feedback from trusted mentors, colleagues, friends, or family members. Constructive feedback provides valuable insights into your progress and areas for improvement. It also helps you gain an external perspective on your abilities. Be open to both praise and constructive criticism, as they contribute to your growth and self-trust. Constructive feedback from trusted individuals can also help you refine your skills and gain confidence in your abilities.**Exercise 3: Face Your Fears**

**Fear Journal:** Create a dedicated journal where you list your fears and anxieties as they arise. Next to each fear, write a counterargument or an action plan. This exercise encourages you to confront your fears rationally. For example:

1. Fear: Public speaking in front of a large audience

2. Counterargument: I have prepared extensively for this presentation and know the topic well.

3. Action Plan: Practice public speaking in front of a smaller group first to build confidence.

**Fear-Challenging Activities:** Regularly engage in activities that challenge your fears or insecurities. Whether it's public speaking, socializing in new settings, confronting a phobia, or taking on a new role or responsibility, facing your fears head-on builds self-trust. When you confront a fear and realize you can handle it, your self-trust strengthens. Start with smaller challenges and progressively tackle more significant ones as your confidence grows.

**Fear of Failure Reflection:** Embrace failure as a learning opportunity. After experiencing a setback or failure, instead of dwelling on self-doubt, reflect on what you've learned from the experience. Ask yourself questions like:

- What specific factors led to this setback or failure?

- How can I use this knowledge to avoid similar mistakes in the future?

- What adjustments can I make in my approach or strategy to succeed next time?

By framing failures as opportunities for growth and learning, you shift your perspective and reinforce your trust in your ability to navigate challenges effectively.**Exercise 4: Practice Self-Compassion**

**Self-Kindness Letters:** Create a practice of writing yourself letters of kindness and encouragement. When you face self-doubt, criticism, or moments of low self-trust, read these letters to remind yourself of your worth and potential. In these letters:

- Acknowledge your strengths, achievements, and positive qualities.

- Offer yourself words of comfort and reassurance during challenging times.

- Express belief in your ability to overcome obstacles and thrive.

These self-kindness letters serve as a source of comfort and motivation, fostering self-compassion and self-trust.

**Mindfulness Meditation:** Incorporate mindfulness meditation into your daily routine. Mindfulness meditation encourages you to observe your thoughts and feelings without judgment. This practice can help you become aware of self-doubt and self-criticism as they arise. Instead of reacting negatively to these thoughts, observe them with detachment and self-compassion. Over time, this practice can help you cultivate self-compassion and self-trust by allowing you to distance yourself from unhelpful, self-critical thinking patterns.

**Positive Self-Talk:** Pay close attention to your inner dialogue. Whenever you engage in self-critical or self-doubting thoughts, consciously redirect your internal dialogue. Replace these negative thoughts with affirmations of self-compassion and self-trust. For example:

- Replace self-doubt with: "I trust myself to make the right choices."

- Replace self-critical thoughts with: "I am worthy of love, acceptance, and success."

This practice gradually transforms your self-talk, fostering self-trust from within.

**Exercise 5: Strengthen Intuition**

**Quiet Reflection:** Dedicate time each day to quiet reflection. Find a peaceful environment, close your eyes, take deep breaths, and center your focus on your intuition. Pay attention to the thoughts, feelings, or inner nudges during this time. What is your inner wisdom trying to communicate to you? Over time, this practice helps you become more attuned to your intuitive signals, strengthening your trust in your inner guidance.

**Gut Feeling Journal:** Start and maintain a journal dedicated to your intuition. Whenever you encounter situations where you followed your gut feeling, regardless of whether the outcome was positive or negative, document them. Reflect on the accuracy of your intuition. Were there times when you ignored your intuition and later wished you hadn't? By reviewing these instances, you gain insights into the reliability of your intuition and learn to trust it more readily.

**Ask for Intuitive Guidance:** When faced with important decisions, converse with yourself to seek intuitive guidance. Trust your initial instincts and gut feelings. Avoid second-guessing yourself unless there's concrete evidence to justify doing so. This practice empowers you to rely on your intuition as a valuable decision-making tool and builds self-trust in your inner wisdom.

**Exercise 6: Set and Achieve Goals**

**SMART Goals:** When setting goals, adopt the SMART framework—Specific, Measurable, Achievable, Relevant, and Time-bound. Creating clear and structured goals that meet these criteria makes it easier to trust yourself to achieve them. SMART goals provide a roadmap for your actions, enhancing your belief in your ability to progress towards your desired outcomes.

**Celebrate Achievements:** Cultivate the habit of celebrating your successes, no matter how small they may seem. Acknowledging and celebrating your accomplishments reinforces your belief in your ability to achieve more significant goals. Recognize the effort, dedication, and perseverance you invest in your goals. Celebration is a powerful motivator and a reminder of your competence and self-trust.

**Learn from Setbacks:** Embrace setbacks as opportunities for growth rather than failures. When you encounter obstacles or experience setbacks in your pursuit of goals, take the time to analyze what went wrong. What factors contributed to the setback, and how can you adjust your approach? By viewing setbacks as learning experiences, you build resilience and deepen your trust in your problem-solving abilities.

### Exercise 7: Cultivate a Support System

**Identify Trusted Allies:** Identify friends, family members, or mentors who believe in you and support your journey to enhance self-trust. Seek their guidance and encouragement when needed. Trusted allies can provide valuable insights, advice, and emotional support, reinforcing your belief in your capabilities.

**Share Your Goals:** Don't hesitate to share your goals, aspirations, and challenges with those you trust. Communicating your ambitions makes you more accountable and creates a support network. Sharing your journey with others holds you responsible for your actions and allows you to receive encouragement and feedback, bolstering your self-trust.

**Mutual Support:** Offer support and encouragement to others on their journeys to self-trust. Being part of a supportive community can strengthen your own self-trust. When you encourage others to pursue self-trust and authenticity, you deepen your understanding of these concepts and reinforce their importance in your own life. Mutual support creates a positive feedback loop, benefitting everyone involved.

Building self-trust is a dynamic and ongoing process. It requires patience, self-compassion, and consistent effort. The practical exercises and activities provided in this book help nurture and reinforce your self-trust across various aspects of your life. As you embark on your journey of self-discovery and growth, remember to regularly revisit and adapt these exercises to your specific needs and evolving circumstances. Over time, you will find that your self-trust deepens and becomes an integral part of navigating the world and living authentically.

## Appendix B: Additional Resources

Building self-trust is a lifelong journey, and many valuable resources are available to support you on this path. Whether you're looking for books to deepen your understanding, websites for ongoing guidance, or communities where you can connect with like-minded individuals, this list of additional resources will help you continue your journey towards greater self-trust and authenticity:

**Books:**

1. **"The Gifts of Imperfection" by Brené Brown:** In this book, Brené Brown explores the importance of vulnerability, self-compassion, and embracing imperfections as keys to living a wholehearted life.

2. **"Daring Greatly" by Brené Brown:** Brown delves into the power of vulnerability and how it connects to self-trust and courageous living.

3. **"Mindset: The New Psychology of Success" by Carol S. Dweck:** Learn about the concept of a growth mindset and how it can help you build confidence and resilience.

4. **"Radical Acceptance" by Tara Brach:** Tara Brach offers insights on embracing yourself fully and cultivating self-compassion through mindfulness practices.

5. **"The Power of Now" by Eckhart Tolle:** Explore the concept of living in the present moment and how it can lead to greater self-trust and inner peace.

6. **"The Four Agreements" by Don Miguel Ruiz:** Discover the four agreements that can guide you towards personal freedom, self-trust, and authentic living.

7. **"The Gifts of Imperfection" by Marianne Williamson:** This book provides spiritual guidance on embracing your authentic self and living with self-trust.

**Websites:**

1. **Mindful.org:** Mindful.org offers many resources and articles on mindfulness, self-compassion, and personal growth.

2. **Psychology Today:** Psychology Today's website is a valuable source for articles and expert insights on building self-trust, self-compassion, and mental well-being.

3. **Greater Good Magazine:** This online publication from the Greater Good Science Center at UC Berkeley explores the science of well-being, including self-compassion and resilience.

4. **Tiny Buddha:** Tiny Buddha is a community-driven website that offers articles, stories, and practical advice on mindfulness, self-trust, and personal development.

5. **The Center for Self-Compassion:** Created by Dr. Kristin Neff, this website provides resources and exercises to help you develop self-compassion, a vital component of self-trust.

**Supportive Communities:**

1. **Meetup.com:** Search for local or online meetup groups focused on self-improvement, personal development, and mindfulness. Joining such groups can provide a sense of community and support.

2. **Online Forums and Facebook Groups:** Look for forums or groups dedicated to self-trust, personal growth,

and mindfulness. These communities provide a space for discussion, sharing experiences, and seeking advice.

3. **Local Meditation or Mindfulness Groups:** Many communities have meditation or mindfulness groups that meet regularly. Participating in these groups can help you connect with like-minded individuals and deepen your practice.

4. **Therapist or Counselor:** Consider seeking the guidance of a therapist or counselor who specializes in self-esteem, self-trust, and personal development. They can provide personalized support and strategies.

5. **Workshops and Retreats:** Explore workshops, seminars, and retreats in your area or online that focus on self-trust, self-compassion, and personal growth. These immersive experiences can be transformative.

Remember that your journey towards greater self-trust is unique, and it's okay to explore various resources and communities to find what resonates with you. Continuously learning and seeking support from others can be powerful tools as you navigate the beautiful path towards living authentically and trusting yourself fully.

## About the Author

**Dr. Michael J. Duckett** is a world-renowned social scientist, speaker, and author of numerous books and programs. His focus is on human achievement, habits, and thought patterns. His work has been credited with positively helping millions of people's lives. Dr. Duckett is a former college professor, researcher, and lifetime student with numerous advanced degrees. He currently lives in Atlanta, Georgia, with his family.

For more information on Dr. Duckett, please visit one of his websites online. Additionally, he has numerous free YouTube videos available to the general public. Many of Dr. Duckett's books and programs can be found on Amazon.com.

Websites:

Upgradinglife.com

Professionalincomesolutions.com

Fastcoachtraining.com

# ABOUT THE AUTHOR

**Dr. Michael J. Duckett** is a world-renowned social scientist, speaker, and author of numerous books and programs. His focus is on human achievement, habits, and thought patterns. His work has been credited with positively helping millions of people's lives. Dr. Duckett is a former college professor, researcher, and lifetime student with numerous advanced degrees. He currently lives in Atlanta, Georgia, with his family.

For more information on Dr. Duckett, please visit one of his websites online. Additionally, he has numerous free YouTube videos available to the general public. Many of Dr. Duckett's books and programs can be found on Amazon.com.

Made in the USA
Columbia, SC
29 January 2025

52975161R00091